$\big($ GREAT CHRISTIAN THINKERS $\big)$

Francis & Bonaventure

PAUL ROUT

Paul Rout is a member of the Franciscan
Order of Friars Minor. He graduated from
the University of Melbourne and continued
postgraduate study at Heythrop College,
University of London. His doctoral thesis,
on Bonaventure and the religious experience of Francis of Assisi, was recently accepted by the University of London. Dr Rout
presently lectures in Philosophy and
Franciscan Studies at the Franciscan Study
Centre, Canterbury, England.

The series editor, Dr Peter Vardy, is lecturer
in the Philosophy of Religion at Heythrop
College. He is a former Chair of the
Theology Faculty Board of the University
of London. Among his previous books are
The Puzzle of God, *The Puzzle of Evil*, *The
Puzzle of Ethics* and *The Puzzle of the Gos-
pels*.

D0907915

Praise for Other Titles in the Great Christian Thinkers Series

AUGUSTINE Richard Price
'... admirably clear, concise, and though sometimes critical, written with great sympathy and understanding of Augustine's problems, and of the historical context within which he was labouring.' MICHAEL WALSH, *BUTLER'S LIVES OF THE SAINTS* AND *BOOK OF SAINTS*

FRANCIS & BONAVENTURE Paul Rout
'This book meets a real need ... a painless way into Bonaventure's life and thinking, both as a philosopher, a man of prayer and as a great Franciscan.' SISTER FRANCES TERESA, OSC, THE COMMUNITY OF THE POOR CLARES, ARUNDEL

JOHN OF THE CROSS Wilfrid McGreal
'We are greatly indebted to Fr Wilfrid McGreal for bringing alive in such an accessible way the mysticism and mystery of St John of the Cross.' GEORGE CAREY, ARCHBISHOP OF CANTERBURY

THOMAS MORE Anne Murphy
'This superb piece of scholarship sheds new light on the enduring importance of the unity between Thomas More's life and thought. Anne Murphy shows how this large-hearted Christian was a great European and an outstanding example of personal and public integrity.' GERALD O'COLLINS, GREGORIAN UNIVERSITY, ROME

KIERKEGAARD Peter Vardy
'This is a fascinating introduction to Kierkegaard's prophetic insights into the nature of Christian faith, insights which we desperately need to ponder today.' GERALD HUGHES, AUTHOR OF *GOD OF SURPRISES*

SIMONE WEIL Stephen Plant
'Stephen Plant portrays the immense strength and the touching vulnerability of Simone Weil, the complex nature of her convictions, and the startling and continuing relevance of her views today.' DONALD ENGLISH, CHAIRMAN OF THE WORLD METHODIST COUNCIL

FRANCIS & BONAVENTURE

Paul Rout

SERIES EDITOR: PETER VARDY

Triumph
Liguori, Missouri

Published by Triumph
An Imprint of Liguori Publications
Liguori, Missouri

Library of Congress Cataloging-in-Publication Data

Rout, Paul.
    Francis & Bonaventure / Paul Rout. — 1st U.S. ed.
       p.   cm. — (Great Christian thinkers)
    Includes bibliographical references and index.
    ISBN 0-7648-0113-9
    1. Francis, of Assisi, Saint, 1182–1226. 2. Bonaventure, Saint, Cardinal, ca.
1217–1274. I. Title. II. Series.
BX4700.F6R68   1997
282'.092'2—dc21
[B]   96-52492

Originally published in English by HarperCollinsPublishers Ltd under the title: *Francis and Bonaventure* by Paul Rout.

First U.S. Edition 1997
01 00 99 98 97   5 4 3 2 1
Printed in the United States of America

To my family
Cecilia, Frank, Terry, Brian and Kevin
and to my Franciscan brothers and sisters.

Contents

Abbreviations

The following abbreviations are used in references to Bonaventure's works in the text:

B   *Breviloquium* (*The Breviloquium*)
H   *Collationes in Hexaemeron* (*Collations on the Six Days*)
I   *Itinerarium Mentis in Deum* (*The Soul's Journey into God*)
L   *The Life of St Francis* (*Legenanda Maior*)
SC *Disputatae Quaestiones de Scientia Christi* (*Disputed Questions on the Knowledge of Christ*)
T   *De Triplica Via alias Incendium Amoris* (*The Triple Way or Love Enkindled*)

Details of editions cited are given in Suggested Further Reading

Date Chart

Introduction

The medieval world of the thirteenth century was one of enormous social, cultural and religious change. Previous certainties were being questioned, controversies arose within political, academic and church circles. Within the hearts of many arose a new spiritual hunger which the traditional religious authorities seemed unable to assuage.

Into this world leapt one of God's special gifts to humanity, one who breathed with every fibre of his being a joy which could not be taken away, a peace which sank deep into the hearts of those whom he encountered. This man came from the Umbrian city of Assisi and his name was Francis. His life was living poetry. He was enthralled by God, the Divine Lover, and he lived out the reality of that relationship passionately, freely and joyfully.

Yes, Francis was captivated by God's love. This was the secret of his freedom, a freedom which put flight to fear and opened his heart to love in return. His was indeed a passionate love, one which reached out to embrace all his sisters and brothers, especially the lost ones, the outsiders, the poor and insignificant. It was a love, moreover, which extended to all of creation, which Francis saw as radiant with reflections of the divine glory.

The life and spirit of the little poor man of Assisi intensely affected the lives of so many of his contemporaries, people from all walks of life. One such person was Bonaventure. It might seem at first sight that Bonaventure would be far removed from the attractions of Assisi. He was the brilliant academic, the Master at the

University of Paris. The power and prestige of the academic world lay at his feet, and yet he chose to follow the way of Francis. His powerful intellect was energetically put to the task of relating the significance of the Francis-event to the concerns of the wider world. Bonaventure reflected on Francis' experience and, in a unique and powerful testimony to that experience, he produced works of theology which are permeated with the spirit of love, prayer and reverence which overflowed within the heart of Francis.

Francis stands as one who began with God and saw all else from there. Bonaventure's writings provide a Francis-inspired guide for the spiritual pilgrim, the one who is seeking God. It is a journey which is dynamic and relational. It is a journey which speaks so profoundly of the reality of God within our lives and of the meaning which God alone is able to provide for the concerns of human life. It is a journey which embraces this world and which emphasizes the dignity and sacredness of all creation. The spiritual journey of Francis and Bonaventure is not simply a record from the past. It is one which can continue to offer nourishment to spiritual pilgrims of our own day. It is hoped that this short book will open the door so that the reader may set out with confidence and with a joyful heart along the fascinating road of the journey into God.

Francis and Bonaventure in Context

*Indeed, not so much of the water of philosophy should be mixed with
the wine of Revelation that it should turn wine into water. This should
be the worst of miracles. We read that Christ turned water into wine,
not the reverse.* (H 19.14)

The relationship between revelation and philosophy is no less
an area of debate in our own time than in that of Bonaventure.
Revelation involves God making known truths about himself and
the universe to human beings. Philosophy, on the other hand, is a
process whereby human beings use processes of logic to determine fundamental truths. In the thirteenth century medieval
world of the University of Paris, controversy stirred in the academic faculties. The 'new learning' which had filtered into the universities carried with it a heavy influence from the recently
discovered philosophical texts of Aristotle. Aristotle's philosophy
was accepted as an essential element of University learning the
controversy surrounded the proper place of such philosophy
within the academic process.

On the one side were those who saw in Aristotle a means whereby human reason would be 'set free' from the strictures of church
tradition to think for itself. For example, Siger of Brabant (1240
–1284) separated revelation and philosophy, insisting on the right
of the philosopher to follow human reason to its inevitable conclusions, even though it might sometimes contradict revelation. Religious faith was not to be dismissed, but its concepts were to be

subject to the analysis of reason. Aristotelian philosophy, with its emphasis on the self-sufficiency of human reason, would bring about this liberation. Philosophy, not theology and religious tradition, would set the agenda for the new world.

Numbered among scholars who opposed such a stance was Bonaventure. In his mind, to separate philosophy from theology within university learning was to deprive human reason of that which made for its greatness, namely, the influence of divine revelation, the subject matter of theology. Bonaventure was convinced that reflection on the nature of human life could only take place within the context of reference to God as the origin and fulfilment of human destiny. To attempt to reason apart from this context, he claimed, was to deprive life of its essential vitality, a vitality which could be found only in God.

Bonaventure's stance was not due to mere academic preference. Just as the academic world of the thirteenth century had been heavily influenced by Aristotle, so the religious and social world had been unalterably shaken by the life of one man – not a philosopher but a poet, a mystic, a saint – Francis of Assisi. Bonaventure had been so affected by the story of this man that in Paris he entered the Order which Francis had founded. It was because of the experience of Francis that Bonaventure held to his academic conviction. He saw Francis as embodying truth and believed that this embodiment of truth was only possible because of Francis' experience of the transcendent God. To consider Francis outside of this experience, he affirmed, would be as life-giving as to change wine into water. Bonaventure understood Francis to have begun with God and to have reflected on all else in relation to that starting point. Similarly, he would insist, it was to be the truth of God breaking into human life which was to determine the truth of human thought; it was not human thought which was to determine the truth of God.

Bonaventure, the intellectual giant of Paris; Francis, the little poor man of Assisi. Miles apart, it would seem, yet their lives and destinies are inextricably linked in history. Indeed, it could be argued that it is because of the later events in Paris that the medieval spirit of Assisi survives and is of such relevance for today's religious and social world. This book will introduce the reader to the life and religious genius of St Francis and to the theological and philosophical reflection on that life which is to be found in the writings of Bonaventure. It will also suggest that from this medieval Franciscan experience, the contemporary world can draw much inspiration when seeking to address many of the pressing concerns of our own time.

Francis, the Poor Man of Assisi

Francis was born in the Umbrian town of Assisi in 1182. His father was a wealthy clothing merchant, and it seemed for some years that Francis was to play the role of the rich father's son. He is reported to have been the star of Assisi's young social set, and his natural exuberance found expression in pursuing a lifestyle which his wealth and social position enabled him to enjoy to the full. He dreamed of glory as a knight, and at twenty years of age set off to battle for Assisi in the war against the neighbouring city of Perugia. Francis' dream, however, took an unexpected turn. Taken captive in battle, Francis spent a year in prison in Perugia, a year which led him to reflect deeply on the direction of his life. His return from Perugia after his father had paid the ransom for his release was followed by a lengthy illness. His recovery took twelve long months, after which he sought to resume his earlier lifestyle. He set out once more for war in Apulia. But now the stirrings within him reached their crisis point. Francis realized he could no longer resist the changes in his way of life which were being called for from the depths of his heart. He could no longer continue to live a lie.

Despite the threat of social disgrace (for it was not proper for a knight to return from battle in this way), he returned to Assisi the very next day. This was to mark the final turning point. Francis was to leave behind family, wealth, social standing and material ambitions and to embark on a journey for which he willingly forsook all else, the journey into the heart of being captivated by God.

It was this experience of Francis, the experience of being overwhelmed and captivated by God's love, that was to transform so radically not only his own life but the religious and social world in which he lived. Francis was led into the most exciting of life's journeys. He became able to accept and even to love those dimensions of life which previously he had feared. In doing this, he gained true freedom. It was a freedom which marked out the path of his life. It enabled him to choose to live in radical poverty. Instead of seeking glory in war and conflict, he gloried in being the bearer of the good news of peace and goodwill, reaching out in compassion to touch the hearts of all. This freedom enabled Francis to embrace and reverence the whole created world. Someone who is in love sees everything which is associated with the loved one in a new light, in a spirit of devotion and appreciative joy. Francis, as the true lover, saw in a new light everything which God, the loved One, had made, and so grew to appreciate, to reverence and to rejoice in the realities of the world. Such was his sympathy for that world that, today, Francis is held up us as the patron saint of ecology. This freedom, which came from an unshakeable conviction that his being was held forever in the embrace of the God of Life, made it possible for Francis to say as he lay dying in 1226, 'Welcome, Sister Death.'

During his lifetime, Francis' irrepressible magnetism attracted followers who grew rapidly in number and were eventually to be recognized in the Church as a religious Order, the Franciscans. Francis was to later compose a Rule of Life for married people and others who were not members of the Order but who were inspired by his way of life. These were identified as the 'Third Order' and are now known as the Secular Franciscan Order. Today, tens of thousands of men and women throughout the world – within religious communities, as married couples or as unmarried – dedicate their lives to striving to capture and to express something of the joyful freedom which characterized the life of Francis, who, in giving away all for the One he loved, discovered that in giving, he was to receive immeasurably more than he could have ever conceived was possible.

Bonaventure, the Master of Paris

When Francis died, Bonaventure was still in his youth. Bonaventure was born John of Fidanza in Bagnoredgio, near Orvieto, in Tuscany around the year 1217. (His birth is dated by some as 1217 and by others as 1221.) There is relatively little historical detail concerning the circumstances of his life, particularly his earlier life. In around 1235, to prepare himself for a future career, he enrolled as a student for the Master's degree at the Faculty of Arts in the great medieval University in Paris. It was there that he would have come in contact with the early Franciscans. The Franciscans had moved into the university environment so as to have access to the academic facilities which, it was felt, would assist them to be more effective in their reforming mission within the Church. In 1236, a notable event took place within the University which would have deeply affected Bonaventure. The renowned Master within the Faculty of Theology, Alexander of Hales, joined the Franciscan brotherhood, and his Chair of Theology went with him. This event was to indicate to the young theology student that the Franciscan Order had indeed been especially inspired by God. As he wrote years later in a 'Letter to an Unknown Master':

I confess before God that the reason which made me love most of all the life of blessed Francis is the fact that it resembles the beginning and the growth of the Church. The Church, indeed, began with simple fishermen, and was enriched later with most illustrious and learned doctors. Thus you may understand the religion of blessed Francis was established, not by the prudence of men, but by Christ, as shown by

God himself. And because the works of Christ do not fail but cease-
lessly grow, it is God who has accomplished this work, since scholars
have not been reluctant to join the company of simple men, heeding
the word of the apostle [1 CORINTHIANS 3:18]: *'If any one of you*
thinks himself wise in this world, let him become a fool, so that he
may come to be wise.'

He was some short time afterwards to follow Alexander's lead, joining the Order and taking the name Bonaventure. His own academic abilities were recognized and he continued his study of theology under Alexander of Hales and later under John of La Rochelle, Odo Rigaldi and William of Meliton. The date of his inception as Master of Theology is disputed, being given as early as 1248 and as late as 1254. Bonaventure continued teaching at the University (Thomas Aquinas was a fellow academic) until 1257. In that year he was called from his position as Master to serve as the seventh Minister General of the Franciscan Order. In 1273, Bonaventure was named Cardinal Bishop of Albano by Gregory X. He died on 15 July 1274 while attending the Council of Lyons.

During his time in Paris, Bonaventure produced a number of academic works on theology. Some of these works will be examined later in this book. After his election to the position of Minister General, his major writings were of a more deeply religious nature. Nowhere is this exemplified more than in his work *Intinerarium Mentis in Deum* (*The Soul's Journey into God*). When Bonaventure became Minister General, the followers of Francis were experiencing considerable difficulty in living out the spirit of their founder. There was considerable tension between those who sought an almost apocalyptic, spiritual interpretation of Francis' message and those who wished to reduce the radical nature of the Franciscan movement and make it more like the already established Orders. Bonaventure's position as Minister General drew him deep into the conflict, and for this reason he withdrew in 1259 into the solitude of the Franciscan holy mount, La Verna, in order to immerse himself more deeply in the spiritual world of the founder.

La Verna is situated some sixty miles to the north of Assisi. In 1213, Count Roland of Chiusi had given the mountain to Francis as a place where Francis could go for periods of solitude and prayer, just as, in the gospels, Jesus used to retire to the mountains to pray. It was during such a period of prayer in September 1224 that Francis, on the heights of La Verna, experienced the stigmata – in his own body were marked the wounds of the crucified Christ. It was here that Bonaventure composed the *Itinerarium* (*The Soul's Journey into God*), which was both the fruit of his earlier theological speculation and the paradigm for all of his later works. This contemplative and mystical work will provide the pattern for much of what is to be said about Bonaventure's unique contribution to Christian thought and practice.

Although history provides us with little detail concerning Bonaventure's personal life, it would appear that he was held in great respect and even affection by his contemporaries. Historical documents which appear to denigrate his role as Minister General of the Order are more the product of the bias of political infighting than of first-hand observation. Certainly the poetry, the artistry, the serenity, the beauty and piety which so often shine forth in the pages of his writings testify to a man who, like Francis, sought to live in peace and harmony with his God, his brothers and sisters and with the entire world of God's creation.

Francis and Bonaventure were both powerful witnesses in word and action to God's presence breaking into our world. It is time now to explore something of the experience which so enthralled Francis' heart and which so deeply affected the lives of Bonaventure and countless others.

The Inspiration: Saint Francis of Assisi

Most High, all-powerful, good Lord
Yours are the praises, the glory, the honour, and all blessing.
To You alone, Most High, do they belong,
and no man is worthy to mention Your name.

With these words Francis of Assisi begins his magnificent 'Canticle of Brother Sun', a song which burst forth from his heart and which reveals the unique nature of his inspiration. It is significant that the first verses of the 'Canticle' are caught up with praise of God, providing the focus of the central place of God in Francis' life. As in the 'Canticle', so in his whole life – Francis began with God and saw all else from there. The early medieval writings concerning Francis, both those which came from his own hand and those which were written by others, reveal him as one who was passionately in love with God and whose whole life was fired by this passion.

The Historical Sources

Much of our information concerning the life of Francis comes from a variety of early biographies termed *Legenda* – in medieval terms, a document to be read in public liturgical gatherings. Foremost among these were Thomas of Celano's *First Life* (1228); Celano's *Second Life* (1247); Bonaventure's *Major Life* and *Minor Life* (both completed before 1263); *Legend of the Three Companions* (first years of the fourteenth century); *Legend of Perugia* (1311); and the *Mirror of Perfection* (1318). Less in the style of history is the popular *Little Flowers of Francis* (composed between 1327 and 1342).

It is important to distinguish between the large collection of Franciscan writings which appeared within the century after the saint's death and those sources which we refer to as the writings of Francis. What we now recognize as the actual writings of Francis are to be found in the critical edition drawn up by Fr Kajetan Esser, OFM, and first published in 1976. Despite Francis' wish to have his letters and writings copied and preserved, many have been lost over the course of history. Nevertheless we have available to us today a collection of 36 separate writings, composed between 1205 and 1226. It would appear that most of the writings were dictated by Francis to a secretary who may have refined his imperfect Latin. Despite this, the writings serve better than do the biographical sources in providing us with a reasonably comprehensive view of Francis' life. They give us considerable insight into the nature of Francis' personal religious experience, into Francis' understanding of his relationship with God and the implications of this for his life in the world.

Francis was not a medieval philosopher who wrote according to abstract reasoning. His nature was more that of the Romantic, the poet, and, at his deepest level, the mystic. To appreciate the heart of Francis, more is required than a technical examination of his words. It is important to be caught up in the flow of the words, in the way that we might surrender ourselves and be caught up in the rhythm and movement of our favourite music. His religious experience is expressed not so much as theology as personal prayer. When Francis provides moral teaching, he does not leave us with a list of legal obligations, but challenges us to make a response which is motivated by love.

Awareness of the Divine

Max Scheler has written of Francis:

Never again in the history of the West does there emerge a figure marked with such a strength of sympathy and of universal emotion as that of St Francis.

Where lies the secret of such strength? It becomes clear in his writings that Francis had a direct awareness of the presence of God in his life. His religious conversion, he claims, was not simply a change in the way that he looked at life. Nor was it something which was brought about through the influence of others. Other people were very important to him and he was certainly one who knew his own mind. Yet, in these critical moments of his life, Francis was convinced that more was involved – he was convinced that his conversion experience was initiated through the action of God breaking into his life and shattering all his preconceptions.

In his 'Testament', dictated shortly before his death, he describes his conversion in terms of contact with a leper. The story is recounted as to how, while Francis was journeying on horseback, suddenly in his path there stood a leper. Francis had always had a revulsion for lepers and describes their presence as something ' ... bitter to me'. Certainly he had no inclination to go and work in caring for the lepers and would journey miles out of his way in order to avoid making any contact. He does not speak about his conversion experience as one of seeking out lepers but in terms of being ' ... led among them'. On being confronted by the leper, his natural instinct urged him to flee; instead he experienced a granting of strength and compassion which enabled him to reach out and physically embrace the leper, to embrace that which he had feared most.

The Lord granted me, Brother Francis, to begin to do penance in this way: while I was in sin, it seemed very bitter to me to see lepers. And the Lord Himself led me among them and I had mercy upon them.

For Francis, the nature of the encounter lay beyond the power of his own capacities; it was something 'granted' to him. He could only explain this experience, an experience which changed his life, through reference to the action of God erupting from beyond into the context of his life. Later in the 'Testament', Francis writes:

And after the Lord gave me brothers, no one showed me what I should do, but the Most High Himself revealed to me that I should live according to the form of the Holy Gospel.

At the time of his conversion Francis was a layman, not a cleric. Within the context of medieval society, this would have created two barriers between the Scriptures – 'the Holy Gospel' – and himself. In the first place, it is most likely that Francis did not have a Bible at his disposal, both for reasons of cost and for reasons of Church discipline. It was to the clergy only that the task of commenting upon the Scriptures was given. Secondly, the Scriptures were available only in Latin. Although Francis had an excellent command of his native Umbrian dialect, it is noted that his Latin was poor. He would most likely have approached the Scriptures through the mediation of a priest or one of the brothers well versed in Latin.

It is tempting to try to explain Francis' conversion experience as the result of the context in which he lived – to argue that the particular social and religious pressures which had been part of his background created within his mind the feeling that God had called him. This is not the way, however, that even at the end of his life, Francis understood his call from God. As is evident from the above passage from the 'Testament', he did not believe that his particular calling by God had been created by somebody interpreting

Scripture for him. It was not as if he had been told by a priest that this was the meaning of the Scriptures and therefore that he should lead a certain way of life. On the contrary, Francis insists, 'No one told me what I should do'. Although he saw his conversion experience as unfolding within the church community and in the light of the Scriptures, the cause of the experience is not ascribed either to the community or to the Scriptures. Rather, his initial experience is referred to the action of God – 'the Most High Himself revealed to me'. This revelation was gradually clarified as he prayed, sought counsel from those he respected and as he heard the gospel read and explained within his church community. Francis believed in the reality of God's initial and personal call, and the meaning of this then unfolded for him within his social and religious environment.

It is important to remember that Francis never felt that his belief that God had called him directly justified him in 'doing his own thing'. He insisted that his conviction should be tested by the wider community of the Church and he sought confirmation of his calling from the Church's representatives – firstly, his local bishop, and later, the Pope in Rome. In 1209, Pope Innocent III approved Francis' Rule of Life. God may call individuals directly but it is very possible for people to be mistaken about the nature of such a call. In recent years we have seen tragic consequences following from the actions of self-labelled 'prophets' who were convinced that God had called them but who refused to submit their conviction for the approval of the wider religious or social community. Francis, however, realized that his calling was not meant to make him greater than God's people, but ever more a part of God's people. Just as yeast achieves its potential not by being separated from the dough but by being immersed within it, Francis immersed himself in the community of the Church and brought it new life.

Reversal of Values

It is this direct awareness of God's presence in his life which is the secret of Francis' strength. His strong sense of divine calling and of the working of God within his life led him to feel an intense yearning for God. He sought liberation from all that estranged him from God, and he found his model in Jesus Christ. Henceforth, his way of life was to be a literal following of Christ – a dying to self, a living for others, a willingness to give all for the sake of the One whose goodness and love were desirable about all else. There was now a reversal of values – what previously had taken prominent place in his affections left him dissatisfied, while a new system of priorities energized his entire being.

Such a reversal of values could only be achieved through radical dependency on the power of God's Spirit. Francis' use of the word 'Spirit' is akin to that of St Paul – a Hebraic sense of the spirit of the human person being seized by the Spirit of God. It was this power which Francis relied upon, not the power of his own efforts. He spoke of the need to live according to the 'Spirit', rather than according to the 'flesh'.

A servant of God may be recognized as possessing the Spirit of the Lord in this way: if the flesh does not pride itself when the Lord performs some good through him.

The 'flesh' is the egotistical self which sees its own end in itself and its own importance. It is the egotistical self which refuses to acknowledge dependency upon God. Francis identified such an attitude as sin, since it was essentially worship of self rather than worship of God. One who lives according to the 'flesh' is caught up in self-love, whereas one whose life is open to the Spirit dies to self and attributes all good to God.

*Blessed is the servant who esteems himself no better when he is praised and exalted by people than when he is considered worthless, simple, and despicable; **for what a man is before God, that he is and nothing more.***

The living experience of the Spirit was crucial for the way of Francis and dictated his concern for God, his fellow human beings and all of God's creation. It is reported that on one occasion some of his brothers asked Francis whether or not they should feed hungry robbers who were coming to them out of the forests asking for bread. Francis urged his brothers to buy bread and wine, to lay out a supper for the robbers and to serve them with humility and good humour. While the robbers were nourishing themselves, the brothers were to gently speak God's word to them, requesting at first no more than that the robbers refrain from striking or harming anyone. This would bring the robbers, said Francis, to be won over by the charity which had been shown them and in this way they would be enabled to gradually change their style of life.

Whatever of the exact historical details of this story, it reflects an important aspect of Francis' character. He was very much aware of the 'robber' dimension within his own life – perhaps his earlier desires to be recognized before others, maybe to dominate others and to have power over them, or even the will to inflict hurt. He was well aware of the negative actualities and possibilities inherent in his own existence. When a brother asked him, 'Father, what do you think of yourself?', he answered,

I know that I am the worst sinner because, if God had shown some criminal all of the mercy he has shown to me, that man would be twice as spiritual as I am.

Francis' approach to the robbers reflected God's approach to him and the 'robbers' within his own life. His experience of God's Spirit had not been one of condemnation, but rather of welcoming patience and hospitality which gradually led him forward to a new way of life. He had been encouraged to accept his deeper self and to be at peace with that self. No longer did he need to prove himself before others, nor to be afraid when others might react to him in a hostile way. It was this experience which was to form the pattern of his teachings on how people ought to relate to one another, and which was to give Francis to the world as a model for peace, forgiveness and reconciliation.

There should not be anyone in the world who has sinned, however much he may possibly have sinned, who, after he has looked into your eyes, would go away without having received your mercy ... And if he should sin thereafter a thousand times before your very eyes, love him more than me so that you may draw him back to the Lord.

An Instrument of Peace

It was as peacemaker that Francis set out to meet Sultan Melek-el-Kamil. The setting was that of the Fifth Crusade and the fierce hostilities between the Christian world and the world of Islam. In 1218 the army of Crusaders landed on the coast of Egypt and laid siege to the city of Damietta. Their opponent was Melek-el-Kamil, Saladin's nephew, a man described as brilliant, highly cultured and religiously devout. In 1219, Francis came to Damietta in the Nile Delta determined to meet him.

A number of accounts exist of the meeting between Francis and the Sultan. What can be said with certainty is that Francis crossed the lines with the intention of seeking to convert the Sultan by preaching and returned unharmed to the Crusader camp. An Arab author of the fifteenth century also indirectly testifies to the encounter between the two men.

One such account is provided by Jacques de Vitry, who wrote while Francis was still alive and who actually met Francis in Damietta. De Vitry speaks of Francis continuing on from Damietta, unarmed, to the camp of the Sultan. On the way, Francis was taken prisoner, but with the proclamation, 'I am a Christian' and with a request to be led to the Sultan, he was taken to appear before Melek-el-Kamil. The Sultan appeared to be fascinated with Francis and listened to his preaching about Christ. Finally he guaranteed a safe passage for Francis back to the Crusader camp.

These records of the meeting would certainly not satisfy our present-day demands for first-hand, video-style news reports. The incident does, however, tell us much about the spirit which shone through Francis. He had come to the Sultan's camp unarmed, the man of peace. He had been able to cast aside the fears and prejudices which pitted armies against armies. In contrast to the crusader, Francis came to the Sultan's camp '... having no other protection than the buckler of faith'. He had left behind the Christian political structure which the Crusade symbolized, to preach the purity of his belief – faith in Christ and in the God revealed in Christ. He challenged the Sultan to do likewise, to go beyond the Muslim political structure in order to come to terms with his own purity of faith. The fact that the Sultan guaranteed Francis a safe return to the Christian camp indicated that Francis had obviously made a deep impression upon him. It was his deep trust in God which provided Francis with the strength to break down political and religious barriers and to become a model for religious dialogue. Such dialogue is a pressing concern of our own time and later in this book we shall return to examine the significance of this encounter more closely.

The Mystical Embrace – God and Creation

It is not possible to capture the spirit of Francis without under-standing something of Francis the mystic. Central to this mysti-cism is a dying to the egotistical self in order to come to fullness of life in God. His mystical journey was indissolubly linked with his following of Christ, whom he believed in as the incarnational presence of God. Francis describes the mystical union in terms of being '...spouses, brothers, and mothers of our Lord Jesus Christ'. The closeness and tenderness of the mystical union is expressed not only in masculine images of fraternity, but also incorporates the images of married love and the intimate bonding between mother and child.

> *We are spouses when the faithful soul is joined to Jesus Christ by the Holy Spirit ... We are brothers when we do the will of His Father Who is in heaven ... [We are] mothers when we carry Him in our heart and body through love and a pure and sincere conscience; we give birth to Him through [His] holy manner of working, which should shine before others as an example.*

Note that Francis uses here the word 'joined' (*conjungitur*), a word often used in the Middle Ages to express the intimate nature of marital relationships. Francis is not writing abstract theology, he is recounting the overwhelming joy of a deeply personal experience. The intensity of his own experience of God bursts forth in the stream of adjectives of praise which follow.

> *Oh, how glorious it is, how holy and great, to have a Father in heaven! Oh, how holy consoling, beautiful, and wondrous it is to have a Spouse! Oh, how holy and how loving, pleasing, humble, peaceful, sweet, loveable, and desirable above all things to have such a Brother and Son.*

The mystical experience of Francis expressed itself in his relationship with all creation. We find this witnessed to in his 'Canticle of Brother Sun'. The 'Canticle', however, is no commitment to pantheism (the belief that there is nothing which is other than God, that the material universe cannot be separated from God). Nor is it mere aesthetic appreciation of the world of nature. What lies at the heart is Francis' claim that the God whom he has personally experienced is at the same time the Creator God whose goodness is reflected in all that has been created.

The major part of the 'Canticle' was composed by Francis towards the end of his life, at a time when he had been suffering from both physical illness and emotional anxiety about the future of his Order. Yet, as he reflected on his own relationship with God, he was overwhelmed by the persistency of God's goodness and this led him to see and experience the reflections of God's goodness in all created elements.

In the 'Canticle' he addresses the created world as 'Brother', 'Sister', 'Mother'. These attributes are not merely poetical personifications but expressions of spiritual relationship. He was able to enter into such a relationship since he respected all created things for the sacredness of the reflections they bore. His conviction that the Creator God is the highest good enabled him to perceive the world as a sacred reality, since it is a reflection of God's goodness. The praises of the 'Canticle' witness to one who was able, even as he lay ill in the Convent of San Damiano, to discern and feel the creative presence of divine love in all around him. Once again, fear was driven from his heart to be replaced with a deep-seated joy and confidence which none could take from him.

Most High, all-powerful, good Lord,
Yours are the praises, the glory, the honour, and all blessing.
To You alone, Most High, do they belong,
and no man is worthy to mention Your name.
Praise be You, my Lord, with all your creatures ...
Praised be You, my Lord, through our Sister Mother Earth, who
    sustains and governs us,
and who produces varied fruits with coloured flowers and herbs ...
Praise and bless my Lord and give him thanks
and serve Him with great humility.

St Francis is recognized today as the patron saint of ecology. In these final years of the twentieth century, the human race is realizing as never before the need to have respect and concern for the natural world in which we live. Without such respect, the ecological balance can be destroyed, resulting in tragic consequences for future generations. It is said that modern human beings often seem to live as strangers to the environment, unable to relate properly to the world in which they live. What Francis offers is the ability to recover the sense of our spiritual relationship with the created world through the conviction that all created entities contain within themselves reflections of God's creative goodness. As Francis' thirteenth-century biographer, Thomas of Celano, wrote in *The Second Life of St Francis*:

> *Francis sought occasion to love God in everything. He delighted in all the works of God's hands and from the vision of joy on earth his mind soared aloft to the life-giving source and cause of it all. In everything beautiful, he saw Him who is beauty itself; and he followed his Beloved everywhere by his likeness imprinted on creation; of all creation he made a ladder by which he might mount up and embrace Him who is all-desirable.*

Bonaventure, in his own major account of Francis' life, comments:

> *When he considered the primordial source of all things he was filled with even more abundant piety, calling creatures no matter how small, by the name of brother or sister, because he knew they had the same source as himself.* (L 8.6)

Francis' ultimate mystical experience occurred on the heights of the holy mountain, La Verna. As was noted in Chapter 1, Francis used to retire to La Verna for lengthy periods of solitude and prayer, and it was here that he experienced in his own body the wounds of the crucified Christ. His death to self in imitation of

Christ reached its fullest expression in this bodily identification with Christ's act of self-giving love in obedience to God. Brother Leo, Francis' close companion who had accompanied him on this occasion to La Verna, wrote:

> *After the vision and words of the Seraph and the impression of the stigmata of Christ in his body he composed these praises written on the other side of this sheet and wrote them in his own hand, giving thanks to God for the kindness bestowed on him.*

> *You are holy, Lord, the only God, You do wonders.*
> *You are strong, You are great, You are the most high,*
> *You are the almighty King.*
> *You, Holy Father, the king of heaven and earth.*
> *You are Three and One, Lord God of gods;*
> *You are good, all good, the highest good,*
> *Lord, God, living and true.*
> *You are love, charity,*
> *You are wisdom; You are humility; You are patience;*
> *You are beauty; You are meekness; You are security;*
> *You are inner peace; You are joy; You are our hope and joy;*
> *You are justice; You are moderation, You are all our riches*
> *[You are enough for us]*
> *You are Beauty, You are meekness;*
> *You are the protector,*
> *You are our guardian and defender;*
> *You are strength; You are refreshment.*
> *You are our hope, You are our faith, You are our charity,*
> *You are all our sweetness,*
> *You are our eternal life:*
> *Great and wonderful Lord,*
> *God almighty, Merciful Saviour.*

Such was Francis' experience of God, an experience which transformed his life and was to set him aside as an inspiration and example for future travellers along the path of the journey to God. One such traveller was Bonaventure. He was to dedicate his God given gifts to expressing for the wider world what it might mean to allow oneself to be seized by the Spirit of God, as had the little poor man of Assisi.

Bonaventure's Intellectual Inheritance

*We should not believe that reading is sufficient without feeling, specu-
lation without devotion, investigation without wonder, observation
without joy, work without piety, knowledge without love, understanding without humility, endeavour without divine grace.* (I PROLOGUE 4)

Many stories and legends were created about Francis, although we
have relatively little remaining of his own writings. With Bonaventure, the reverse is the case. We have quite a large collection of his
own works, but very little written about Bonaventure by those
who knew him. His own writings are those of the scholar – at
times of a technical, philosophical nature, at other times, full of
the freshness and vitality of the poet and the literary genius. As
a scholar he was familiar with a wide range of earlier Christian
and non-Christian thinkers and drew on these to produce a
unique philosophical theology. None the less, the heart of his
inspiration, as we shall see, remained the life and experience of
Francis of Assisi.

Bonaventure's writings can be divided into two categories,
those of the time he spent at the University of Paris and those after
his election to the position of Minister General of the Franciscan
Order. Those which emerged from his period in Paris are in keeping with the accepted later medieval methods of argumentation.
The question under examination is firstly answered in the affirmative and supported with a presentation of arguments from accepted authorities, notably the Church Fathers and the writings of the

philosophers. Objections to this position are then considered, after which the Master puts forward his conclusion. Finally, he replies to the objections earlier raised. We see this structure in works such as *Disputed Questions on the Mystery of the Trinity* and *Disputed Questions on the Knowledge of Christ*. Following his election as Minister General, his writings tend to be of a more spiritual nature. We see notable differences in style and content in later works such as the *Itinerarium* or the *Collations on the Six Days*. He continues, however, to show familiarity with, and to draw upon, the academic authorities which were important in his earlier works.

Who were these academic authorities and in what ways did they influence the shape of Bonaventure's thought? Although Bonaventure drew on a wide range of such authorities, this book will concentrate on three key figures. From the early period of the Church, Bonaventure draws on traditions both from the West and from the East, notably, Augustine and Pseudo-Dionysius. From times closer to his own, he was particularly influenced by the thought of the School of St Victor.

Augustine

The writings of Augustine (AD 354–430) are voluminous and it is well beyond the scope of this book to attempt any critical analysis of them. What can be said, however, is that Bonaventure took from Augustine the fundamental starting point for his theological reflection. It was Augustine who wrote:

> *Believe in order to understand. Faith necessarily comes first and understanding later.*

This did not mean that people who profess to have faith do not need to reason about their faith. For Augustine, it was important to use the God-given gift of human intelligence in order to integrate the faith we profess with the concerns of our life in the world. There was to be no separation between the concerns of religious faith and the concerns of everyday life.

What Augustine wanted to stress, however, is that rational arguments will not produce faith. Faith is a fundamental conviction held by the human person, and no amount of reasoning can bring about such a conviction. Augustine urges that we begin with that conviction and then seek to understand it. This task of understanding will necessarily entail that we rationally reflect on our faith. Theology addresses this task as one of its major concerns. Consequently, Augustine affirms, the Church's theology must begin with the Scriptures, with revelation, the expression of faith convictions which have been handed down through the ages.

Like Augustine, Bonaventure believed that theological reflection must begin with faith. Not faith in the sense of belief in certain propositions, but faith meaning the individual's fundamental conviction that life finds its ultimate meaning and significance in the God who has created this world and who holds and sustains creation in being. The Scriptures or revelation, as the recorded experiences of faith recognized and officially accepted by the Church, were to be the springs from which theological thinking must first draw if it was to be fruitful. Having drawn from that wellspring, theology would then use reason to its fullest capacity. Bonaventure was convinced that when we use our reason with a spirit of humility before the greater knowledge which is the revelation of God, then it is possible to begin to formulate an understanding of faith which will answer the deepest aspirations of the human mind and heart.

Mind and heart – this was the secret of Bonaventure's theology. The terms he used were *intellectus* and *affectus* – intelligence and desire, especially the desire of love. When these combine what is produced is not just intellectual knowledge but wisdom – *sapientia*. Wisdom was, for Bonaventure, the aim of theology. One did not study theology in order to learn facts but in order to become wise. Theology must never be merely an intellectual exercise, it must become integrated into a way of life. This is an important lesson for today as well. Intellectual pursuits can all too easily become isolated from the rest of one's life. This is as true about theology as about any other discipline. What we learn from Bonaventure is that theology fails in its task if it remains a mere academic exercise. Its concerns must include the spiritual, moral and social needs of the human person.

One very important area of inquiry in today's world is the field of psychology, the study of the human person. Augustine was a very early Christian psychologist. It may seem to us, familiar as we are with the language of the Freudians and post-Freudians, that his analysis of the human person is rather primitive. Technically speaking, this is probably so, although this book is again inadequate to give a proper assessment of Augustinian psychology. What Augustine did grasp, however, was an extremely important religious insight – that when we delve into the mystery of the human person, we enter in some way into the mystery of God, since the human person is created in God's image. Indeed, much contemporary spiritual direction is based on this premiss. While Augustine's psychological analysis of the human person may appear a little simplistic, this does not negate the value of his fundamental insight.

In Augustine's writings, we are able to discover the outlines of the inward journey to discover God in the depths of the human psyche. Augustine's starting point is his conviction that the human person is essentially the 'image of God'. So when we look into the self, it is as if we are looking into a mirror in which the light of God shines. Imagine looking into a mirror. It is not the mirror itself that we are focusing upon. What draws our attention, rather, is the light that is reflected in the mirror. In the same way, claims Augustine, when we look into the self we are not focusing upon the self but upon the light of God which is reflected there.

Bonaventure takes up this theme in the *Itinerarium* (*The Soul's Journey into God*), particularly in the third chapter:

> *We enter into our very selves; and we should strive to see God through a mirror. Here the light of Truth glows upon the face of our mind.* (I 3.1)

Chapter 3 of the *Itinerarium* concerns itself with a psychological analysis of the self. It is clear, however, that the journey into God is not to be equated simply with the attainment of self-knowledge. This would be to make a God out of psychoanalysis and to identify the religious quest with the psychological quest. Bonaventure does claim that his path will lead to a clearer understanding of the self – the self will only be fully understood in reference to God, who is its source and its final destiny.

Bonaventure's exhortation to journey into the self is an integral part of the journey into God. Those who wish to make the spiritual journey no doubt ask what it might mean to experience a God who cannot be seen. Bonaventure urges us to reflect on the psychological nature of the human self. Since the self is the image of God, it is possible to draw from those reflections analogies which help us to understand something about God. Reflection on the ability to inquire and to reason, for example, can create an awareness of the natural restlessness of the human heart. It is a part of human nature that we yearn to understand more about life and the world, that we have an unquenchable thirst to discover what is true. In using our ability to reason, we are demonstrating a desire to transcend the limitations of the present moment. We are naturally inclined towards the infinite and therein the life of God is reflected.

Reflection upon the human ability to desire and to love reveals how, in loving, the individual is drawn beyond the self into the mystery of the other. In the wonder of that mystery, says Bonaventure, is reflected the wonder of the mystery of the Eternal Other. It is in this type of reflection on the nature of the self that we can begin to understand something of what it means to experience God.

Augustine's influence is evident in Bonaventure's writings. It is to Augustine that he looks to draw support for his conviction that human life cannot be understood without reference to God and that therefore there ought to be no separation between faith and reason, between theology and philosophy. It is also in Augustine that he finds the psychological model which enables him to expound his further conviction, that it is possible for the human person, made in the image of God, to discover and to experience God. Both of these convictions, however, have their foundational inspiration not in a study of theological volumes but in reflection upon the life experience of the little poor man of Assisi.

Pseudo-Dionysius

Bonaventure not only drew upon the Western tradition of Augustine but also appropriated the spirituality of the East, particularly that found in the collection of writings which has been entitled Pseudo-Dionysius. The true identity of the author is unknown. It would appear that at some stage an attempt had been made to give these writings substantive authority by claiming that they originated from a person who had been in contact with the Apostles, namely, Dionysius the Areopagite, who appears in Acts 17:34. Contemporary research seems to indicate that Pseudo-Dionysius was a Syrian who wrote during the first quarter of the sixth century.

The Pseudo-Dionysian texts draw extensively on imagery taken from Neo-Platonic thought. Neo-Platonism is the name given to a branch of thinking which is generally held to have begun with the thought of the third-century philosopher Plotinus. It is labelled Neo-Platonism because Plotinus, although heavily influenced by the work of the great Greek philosopher Plato, introduced a number of modifications into Plato's thought. This was particularly in order to make provision for some of the thoughts of Plato's student and (later) greatest critic, Aristotle.

Neo-Platonism described all reality as springing from an original source which was labelled 'the One'. All life flowed from the One. This flow of life from the One was called the process of 'emanation'. It accounted for the diversity which is found in life, the fact that things are separate and different. And yet, while we experience the world as diverse, we also have a yearning for unity. Such yearning lies, for example, behind the union of love found in marriage, where two different individuals, who are 'opposites' in so far as they are male and female, become one. For Plotinus, such yearning for unity in the midst of diversity will be fulfilled when everything returns to the One from which it has originated.

The writings of Pseudo-Dionysius reveal this fundamental Neo-Platonic structure, but within a Christian framework. The 'One' becomes the Creator God of the Book of Genesis. The work of creation is an 'emanation' or flowing forth from God. Creation is diverse and so displays various levels. For Pseudo-Dionysius, there are three levels:

- totally spiritual beings – the angels
- beings who are both spiritual and material – humans
- totally material realities – plants, rocks, etc.

Each of these levels are related to one another. The angels serve to communicate God's word to humans (for example, Gabriel communicating God's word to the Virgin Mary at the Annunciation). The material world of nature, since it comes from God, can also teach humans something about God. In this way the different levels of reality, through their inter-relatedness, serve to draw all closer to God. This is what Pseudo-Dionysius terms the operation of a 'hierarchy'.

The word 'hierarchy' comes from two Greek words: *hieros*, meaning sacred, and *arche* meaning source or principle. It basically describes the sacred principles which have been established by God in the work of creation in order to enable life to achieve its proper destiny, which is to return to God, the source of all life. Creation, then, is the emanation from God (and, for Pseudo-Dionysius, an overflow of God's essential goodness). God's creation manifests a hierarchical structure, or an essential inter-relatedness between all things. The purpose of this structure is to enable the proper completion of life's journey, which is the return to God. This return is spoken of in a technical sense as the process of 'divinization'.

Pseudo-Dionysius' vision of God and of creation is one where God is active, not a distant 'Unmoved Mover'. God is intimately involved with creation which is seen as God's free gift, an overflowing of the divine goodness itself. God desires that we should share to our utmost ability in this goodness, that we should become 'God-like'. God desires that we should be divinized through the process of the return to the divine source.

The Dionysian writings recognize that in speaking about returning to God, we are faced with two apparently contradictory notions. On the one hand, as St Paul writes, 'Ever since God created the world his everlasting power and deity have been there for the mind to see in the things he has made' (ROMANS 1:20). On the other hand, as found in the Gospel of John, 'No one has ever seen God' (JOHN 1:18). God can be discovered within creation and yet, at the same time, God is totally beyond all that has been created. Thus, while it seems true that we can say something about God which springs from our human experiences of life and the world, it also remains true that whatever we say can never capture the reality of the God who is essentially beyond all our experiences.

Pseudo-Dionysius addresses this problem by speaking of a 'twofold path' to God. It is possible for us to say something about God by giving God the names found in the Scriptures, names which have been revealed by God and are consequently part of the outpouring of God's goodness. The most prominent of these is that

God *is* goodness. To give God names is to affirm something about God. In saying 'God is good', for example, I affirm that God is not evil. In speaking of God as merciful, I affirm that God is not vindictive. Speaking about God in this way – making affirmative statements about God – is known as 'affirmative' or 'cataphatic' theology. The task of affirmative theology is to point the individual in the right way on the journey of returning to God.

However, since God is also the one who is essentially beyond description, it is not possible to identify God with our notions of goodness or mercy. If God were to be identified with these, then we would be able to understand God. God would cease to be mystery – God would cease to be God. If we wish to continue the journey, we must not stay in the one spot. Affirmative theology is like the setting up of a base camp on the ascent to Everest. It provides strength and sustenance. If we remain in the camp, however, we shall never complete the journey to the summit. We must leave behind the security of the camp and venture into the unknown.

This is the second of the paths which Pseudo-Dionysius speaks about. It is called the way of 'negation'. It means leaving behind the spiritual security which our affirmations about God provide and setting off into the unknown. It is possible to affirm that God is goodness, but God must not be identified with any experience of human goodness. In this sense, God is not goodness. This is not saying that God is therefore evil, the opposite of goodness, rather, it is an insistence that God is not to be equated with any *human* understanding of goodness. God is far greater than anything that we can conceive. The way of negation is a stepping into the darkness, and it calls forth an attitude of total trust. This is the way of negation, also known as the 'apophatic' way.

In chapter 5, we shall see in greater detail how Bonaventure integrated elements of Dionysian thought within the framework of his spiritual theology. Suffice it to say at this stage that in Pseudo-Dionysius, Bonaventure found a ready vehicle for his fundamental convictions. Through Dionysian concepts he was able to express his belief that God is not remote and abstract but a God of active goodness, intimately involved with the world, which is itself an overflow of that goodness. Moreover, the ultimate destiny of human life is to return to God. The return is to be completed through a journey which both affirms the goodness and the diversity of God's creation and yet at the same time moves beyond this to the origin and destiny of all created realities – the life of God.

The School of St Victor

Bonaventure's theological style was further influenced by writings which emerged from the School of St Victor. The Abbey of St Victor had its origins as a small hermitage community on the left bank of the Seine. During the twelfth century, the Abbey community came to be recognized not only as a leader in the efforts to renew monastic discipline but also as a centre of a vigorous, dynamic intellectual life. It was open to the theological developments emerging from the new schools at the University of Paris, and produced two of the leading intellectual figures of the latter part of the twelfth century, Hugh and Richard of St Victor. Bonaventure's Franciscan Master at the University, Alexander of Hales, highly respected the Victorine writings and his student came to share this intellectual devotion.

The Victorine tradition taught that theology must be concerned above all with symbolic representations of the sacred. In the work *In Hierarchiam*, Hugh of St Victor wrote:

It is impossible to represent invisible things except by means of those which are visible. Therefore all theology of necessity must have recourse to visible representations in order to make known the invisible.

What we are caught up with here is the meaning of religious symbols. A symbol is more than a sign. A sign is able to give us certain direct information. The sign of an arrow pointing in a particular direction, for example, will inform people where to go. They do not think any further about the meaning of the arrow. A symbol, on the other hand, confronts those who encounter it and provides food for thought. Consider, for a moment, the ocean as a symbol of God. When the ocean is spoken about in this symbolic sense, we are not being provided with technical information about either God or the ocean. Rather, the reality of the ocean confronts us with its immensity, its seemingly eternal activity, its depth, its power, its serenity – the images appear endless. We are called to pause and to contemplate the ocean, to allow the ocean to engage our imagination and the depths of our own beings. As a religious symbol, the ocean confronts us and, through our engagement with it, can lead to a deeper appreciation of the unfolding mystery of God within the history and circumstances of human life.

Bonaventure very much appreciated the richness of the Victorine symbolic mode of thinking. He employed it to express Francis' vision that all created realities reflect God's goodness. Since creation itself is the outpouring of God's goodness, created entities contain reflections of that goodness and so are able to act as religious symbols. If we approach the created world in a spirit of prayer and contemplation, says Bonaventure, allowing that world to engage our imagination, we shall be able to discern the traces of God's footsteps which will lead us to the One whom our hearts desire. In chapter 2 of the *Itinerarium* he writes:

> We can gather that the whole created world is able to lead the mind of the one who is contemplative and wise to the eternal God. (I 2.11)

We have been looking at a number of the significant influences which affected the nature and style of Bonaventure's theology. None the less, it is not possible to understand Bonaventure simply through an examination of these earlier authorities. Bonaventure not only drew on their thought, he moulded and reshaped it, producing a style of theology which was new and unique. In order to discover the secret which is at the heart of Bonaventurean thought, we need to understand how he fired all that he wrote with the inspiration of the poor man of Assisi, Francis. This will be the concern of the next chapter.

Bonaventure: Master of Paris, Disciple of Assisi

Bonaventure's religious world was deeply influenced by the founder of the Order which he entered. The great contemporary Swiss theologian von Balthasar describes the effect of the Francis-event upon Bonaventure in the following words,

> *When we speak of this event, we have at last mentioned the living, organizing centre of Bonaventure's intellectual world, the thing that lifts it above the level of a mere interweaving of the threads of tradition. Bonaventure does not only take Francis as his centre: he is his own sun and his mission.*

Bonaventure had been deeply impressed in his early years in Paris by the followers of Francis who were students and then Masters at the University. As mentioned in chapter 1, the entry of the great Master of Paris, Alexander of Hales, into the Order had been a catalyst for Bonaventure's own decision to join the Franciscans. No doubt he heard from the Franciscans with whom he associated many stories from the life of Francis. In Bonaventure's inquiring mind and poetic heart there must have developed a passion to understand what had seized and motivated the life of this remarkable man from Assisi.

Shortly after his election as Minister General of the Franciscan Order, Bonaventure went on retreat to the Franciscan holy mount, La Verna, where Francis had experienced the stigmata. It was here that he was to produce the *Itinerarium*, in which the basic pattern for all of his theology is found. The genius of Bonaventure lies in the way he grasps the experience of Francis and gives it philosophical and theological expression. This is what constitutes the uniqueness and value of the Bonaventurean theological method.

The *Itinerarium* is structured around the event of Francis' stigmata, when the wounds of the crucified Christ were imprinted upon Francis' body. As Bonaventure states in the Prologue:

> *While I was there reflecting on various ways by which the soul ascends into God, there came to mind, among other things, the miracle which had occurred to blessed Francis in this very place: the vision of a winged Seraph in the form of the Crucified. While reflecting on this, I saw at once that this vision represented our father's rapture in contemplation and the road by which this rapture is reached.* (I PROLOGUE 2)

The *Itinerarium* is basically a prayerful and reflective meditation which aims to lead the individual towards union with God. As Bonaventure emphasizes in its Prologue and again in the final section, the model for the successful completion of the journey is Francis. In this chapter we shall see the ways in which Francis acts as the inspirational model not only for the *Itinerarium* but for all of Bonaventure's theology.

The Way to God

The first six stages of the *Itinerarium* are spoken of as 'contemplations' or reflections. It could appear that Bonaventure is suggesting that it is possible for us to reason our way to God by, for example, elaborating arguments that will prove by the use of human reason alone that God exists. However, at the beginning of chapter 1, the author makes it clear that human effort by itself is not capable of leading to God. There must be assistance from God if the individual is to progress along the path of the journey:

No matter how much our interior progress is ordered, nothing will come of it unless accompanied by divine aid. Divine aid is available to those who seek it from their hearts. Prayer is the mother and source of the ascent. (I 1.1)

As with the life journey of Francis, Bonaventure's religious journey is not simply an ordered, textbook journey which we can undertake. It involves allowing God to break in from beyond into the reality of our lives, shattering even our most cherished conceptions so that we might be gifted with new vision and a new sense of purpose.

Like Francis, Bonaventure begins with God. In Bonaventure's writings, God is always the God of revelation, the Trinitarian God. But it is important to note the sources Bonaventure draws upon in developing his own understanding of the nature of the Trinity.

Firstly, Bonaventure uses the Trinitarian thinking of Pseudo-Dionysius with a particular purpose in mind. Dionysian thought speaks of an active Trinity. It begins with the conviction that God is the highest good. Goodness must, by definition, find expression – if it were never expressed, it could not be known as goodness. To say that God is the highest good is to say that God must express that goodness without limit. Where is there to be found such an unlimited expression? It cannot be found in the world of creation because, as we are well aware, those expressions of goodness, profound as they may be, are necessarily limited. Dionysian thought, however, speaks of God in terms of an active Trinity. It is within the life of God, within the relations between Father, Son and Spirit, that God's goodness is expressed without limit. God as Trinity did not need to create in order to express the divine goodness. The act of creation is an overflow of this expressive goodness, a free gift from a bountiful God.

But Francis experienced God not only as goodness but also, and perhaps more intensely, as love. It is for this reason that Bonaventure takes care to introduce the thought of Richard of St Victor into his theology of the Trinity. Along with Dionysius, Richard maintained that God is the highest good. But he went on to say that of all that is good, nothing can be said to be a higher good than love. Since it is the nature of God to be the highest good, God must be also the fullness of love. Consequently, argues Richard, there must be a number of persons within the Trinity, since love involves the relation of one to another. There must be more than one person within God, otherwise the communication of love would not be possible. Moreover, the fullness of love is to be found when the love which exists between two persons is shared with a third person. The life of God, then, as the fullness of love, is the life of the unending communication of that love between three persons, Father, Son and Spirit.

In integrating the thought of Richard into his theology of the Trinity, along with that of Pseudo-Dionysius, Bonaventure is able to speak of God not only in terms of expressive goodness but also in terms of a communication of love. In so doing he gives theological form to the experience of Francis. God is the good who is to be desired above all. God is the one who communicates, who reaches out and captivates the human soul in the embrace of love.

Francis was a mystic. When he spoke about his experience of God, he used the language of desire and of love. Bonaventure's theology is similarly mystical in nature. The final stage of the *Itinerarium* is entitled 'On spiritual and mystical ecstasy in which rest is given to our intellect when through ecstasy our affection passes over entirely into God'. Here we find the two prominent features of Bonaventurean mysticism, namely, that 'the intellect' is 'given rest', and that it is desire and love which finally lead the soul into God.

It is in keeping with the inspiration which Bonaventure received from Francis that he gives primacy to love. This is not to say that he downgrades the intellect, ignoring the place of rational reflection. The first six stages of the *Itinerarium* witness to the religious value of the exercise of human reason. But in so far as the final stage of the journey moves beyond rational reflection, the affective or emotional is ultimately pre-eminent:

> *In this passing over, if it is to be perfect, all intellectual activities must be left behind and the height of our affection must be totally transferred and transformed into God.* (I 7.4)

In this final stage, to experience God is not to think about our concepts of God, it is to directly encounter God in affective experience. As in the writings of Francis, the imagery Bonaventure uses for the movement towards the mystical state is that of marital love:

> *When it sees its Spouse and hears, smells, tastes and embraces him, the soul can sing like the bride. No one grasps this except him who receives, since it is more a matter of affective experience than rational consideration.* (I 4.3)

This conviction that love is to be the motivating power in the journey to God shines forth in Bonaventure's writings. In *The Triple Way* he writes,

> *Through love, whatever we lack is given to us; through love, an abundance of all good is given to the blessed; and through love, there is attained the supremely desirable presence of the Spouse.* (T 1.16)

It is this same love which is to be found at the heart of Francis' mystical experience of the stigmata. The stigmata are described in terms of the appearance of 'a winged Seraph in the form of the Crucified'. The Seraphs are to be found in the Dionysian writings on the angels. They exist at the highest level of the angelic hierarchy and their function is simply and totally to love God. Francis' stigmata, then, are fundamentally his experience of the overwhelming love of God and also the confirmation of his own love for God. It is in such an experience of divine love, Bonaventure asserts, that ultimate truth is to be found. As he writes in *The Triple Way*, 'Truth is to be embraced with caresses and love as pertains to the Seraphim' (T 3.14).

Even within the more technical of Bonaventure's writings, it is possible to discern a theological approach which is shaped and inspired by his reflections on Francis' experience of God. Towards the end of his tenure as Master at the University of Paris, Bonaventure produced the work *Disputed Questions on the Mystery of the Trinity*. Question 1 of the *Mystery of the Trinity* examines the issue 'Concerning the Certitude with which the Existence of God is Known'.

In his treatment of the topic, Bonaventure is concerned to demonstrate that it is possible for the human person to know God – his concern is experiential. His starting point is his conviction that God exists as the highest good and that the world is God's creation. Through his reflections upon Francis of Assisi's experience of God, he seeks to make this religious reality evident for us. That God *is*, Bonaventure surmises, is evident in the experience of Francis. If there were no God, the life of Francis would have no meaning. It would be irrational and without significance. But Francis, Bonaventure is convinced, does have meaning and significance for human life, and consequently so does the God who is at the centre of Francis' inspiration. Since God *is*, Bonaventure claims, and since the world and all it contains is God's creation, it is possible for us, as it was for Francis, to discover God's presence and so to desire, know and experience God.

Question I discusses ways in which we can come to know of God's existence. For example, in what he calls the 'second way', Bonaventure urges reflection upon the nature of the world as it is experienced. Such reflection will create an awareness of both the experience of limitation and the desire for perfectibility. This is the sort of awareness that we have in times of great happiness – 'I wish this could last for ever ...' And sadly, it does not last for ever. Bonaventure notes this limited nature of our experience. He then argues that we are only aware of limitation because it is possible for us to conceive of the state of perfection – 'This would be just perfect if...' We have the capacity, if not for perfection itself, at least to know what would constitute perfection. Consequently, the argument moves on, we have the capacity to know God who is absolute perfection.

Bonaventure's 'ways' are not attempts at natural theology; that is, they do not aim to logically prove from verifiable premisses that God exists in reality. Bonaventure is not claiming that his arguments would, for example, prove to someone who does not believe in God that God does really exist. He begins with the conviction of faith, the conviction that it is possible to experience the God who is spoken about in the Scriptures. This has been shown in the life and experience of Francis of Assisi. His life was such a powerful testimony and Bonaventure insists that it cannot make sense unless the God whom Francis claimed to have experienced actually exists.

In his theology, Bonaventure's intention is to lead us to say, 'Yes! Even though I cannot logically prove to a non-believer that God exists and that it is possible for us to experience God, I can see that God's existence does make sense for my life as a thinking human being, just as it made so much sense in the life of St Francis.' Bonaventure's theological approach to the question of God cannot be properly understood without the recognition that it is shaped and inspired by Francis' experience of God.

The Created World

The relationship which Francis experienced with God carried over into his relationship with all of creation. Captivated by God's goodness, he rejoiced in and reverenced the world around him since it constantly reminded him of the goodness of God from whom creation flowed. His 'Canticle of Brother Sun' provides ample testimony to this. Bonaventure's writings on the nature of the created world once again express in theological concepts what Francis experienced. Bonaventure presents a theology of creation which emphasizes the inherent goodness and sanctity of all created realities while at the same time directing us beyond those realities to the source of all creation, God.

In the first place, creation is both good and sacred since it flows or 'emanates' from God. Bonaventure employs the Dionysian concept of emanation which was discussed in the previous chapter. His vision of creation is expressed through the image of the life-giving flow of a river. In the thirteenth Collation of *Hexaemeron* he writes,

> *It is written in Ecclesiastes: 'All rivers go to the sea, yet never does the sea become full. To the place where they go, the rivers keep on going. They derive from the sea, and they return to it.'* (H 13.4)

The river is a powerful image of creation. It is the life-giving stream which comes forth from the limitless sea, the image for the bountiful and fertile life of God. Creation, then, has its origin in the action of God which constantly bestows life. The river flows through the earth, and, in the same way, the act of creation involves a journey through history. Just as the river finally returns to the sea, its source of life, so too is the journey of human history to find its completion in being reunited with its origin, the depths of the life-giving mystery of God.

Bonaventure sees the created world as having a sacred purpose. It is given to humanity as a 'home' and it is to serve humanity by awakening within the human spirit 'the fire of love' for God who is the Creator of all. Humanity, then, must respect and care for the created world, in the same way as we respect and care for the home in which we live.

> *All material things exist to serve humanity by enkindling in human beings the fire of love and praise for the one who has made all things*

and by whose providence all things are governed. They have been formed as a sort of home for humanity by the supreme architect until such time as humanity should arrive at that 'house not made by human hands'. (B 2.4)

The world is able to awaken within us the noblest qualities of love, peace, reverence, thanksgiving. As such, it is to be contemplated with reverence and not exploited for selfish purposes. Such was the attitude of Francis towards his world, a world with which he entered into a spiritual relationship, a world in the midst of which he rejoiced and walked in freedom because it spoke to him constantly the language of God's love and goodness. So it is with Bonaventure – it is the awareness of 'spiritual relationship' that must mark the interaction between humanity and the natural environment.

Francis' awareness of the sacred dignity of the created world finds further theological expression in Bonaventure's use of the term 'exemplarism'. An exemplar is an original model. Exemplarism is the process whereby likenesses are created of the original model. In artistic terminology, we could speak of the exemplar as, for example, the original painting of a Great Master. Exemplarism would be the process whereby prints of the original are produced. The prints are not the original but they are likenesses of the original. Bonaventure speaks metaphorically of God as the Divine Artist. The original 'model of God' (we are speaking here metaphorically) is the Trinity. The Trinity is the eternal exemplar. In the work of creation, the divine artist produces 'prints' of the original masterpiece. All created realities contain, in some way, likenesses of the Trinity. Moreover, to continue the artistic analogy, when we contemplate the work of an artist, we are able to learn something about the artist. The artist is expressed in some way in the work of art. For Bonaventure, the world is God's work of art. As such it expresses the life of its author and therefore contains within itself reflections of the life of God, the life of the Trinity. In contemplating

God's works of art, therefore, we are able to learn something about God. As Bonaventure writes in the *Breviloquium*, 'The created world is like a book in which its Maker, the Trinity, shines forth, is represented, and can be read' (B 2.12).

Human History – The Search for Harmony

Created reality is, for Bonaventure, essentially Trinitarian in structure. Like the Trinity, creation is diverse and we are well aware of its diversity. We are also aware that the experience of diversity can sometimes lead to conflict. When people are confronted by the 'other' who is different, the temptation can be either to destroy the other or to attempt to assimilate the other and to make the other the same. Bonaventure's Trinitarian vision of life, however, presents a compelling alternative. Within the Trinity, there is diversity, the opposites of Father and Son. Yet these opposites do not conflict, nor do they seek to make the other the same. They remain fully as opposites and yet exist in perfect harmony through the mediation of the Spirit, the breath of love and goodness which flows between Father and Son.

For Bonaventure, God contains at one and the same time both the harmony of Unity and the individuality of Trinity. Within the Trinity, the individual Persons are fully individual and different, yet are in harmony through the mediation of divine love. In the very depths of the life of God, unity exists in and through diversity. This is possible since the life of the Trinity is the life of active goodness in which are found relationships of love. These, then, are the qualities which should mark life in the world, life which is characterised by the experience of life's diversity, but which also yearns for unity and harmony. The human journey through history is to be a journey of reconciliation. It is to be a journey which recognizes the unique individuality of each and every human being while at the same time being actively involved in the task of peace-making. And again, the model for the journey is Francis, the Man of Peace.

I call upon the Eternal Father to guide our feet in the way of that peace which surpasses all understanding. This is the peace proclaimed and given to us by our Lord Jesus Christ and preached again and again by our father Francis. At the beginning and end of every sermon he announced peace; in every greeting he wished for peace; in every contemplation he sighed for ecstatic peace. (I PROLOGUE 1)

Bonaventure speaks of the journey of human history in terms of the image of the circle. In tracing a circle, the circle returns to its point of origin. The journey is complete when the circle is complete, when the return to the origin is accomplished. At the conclusion of his work on the Trinity, Bonaventure writes:

Eternal life consists in this alone, that the human person, who emanates from the most blessed Trinity and is a likeness of the Trinity, should return after the manner of a certain intelligible circle to the most blessed Trinity by God-conforming glory. (T 8 REPLY 7)

Yet we find from the experience of life that harmony and unity are not yet attained. The circle of harmony has not been completed. Bonaventure insists that it is impossible for humanity to complete the circle by itself. Humanity is lost, the circle of harmony has been broken and the centre of the circle cannot be found in order to complete the circle. It is here that God takes the initiative. God locates the centre for us. And how, asks Bonaventure, is the centre of the circle to be found?

How marvellous is divine wisdom, for it brought forth salvation through the cinders of humility. For the centre is lost in the circle, and it cannot be found except by two lines crossing each other at right angles. (H 1.24)

The two lines crossing each other at right angles stand for the crucified Christ. It is in Christ that we are put at rights once more.

When a life is centred around Christ, when it is Christ-like, the journey into God is renewed and the harmony for which the human spirit longs is restored.

The circle and the centre are no mere theological abstractions for Bonaventure. Once again, Francis is his inspiration. It is significant that Francis' religious journey began as he knelt alone in prayer before the Crucifix in the Church of San Damiano. It was here that Francis heard the words which were to motivate his life. Bonaventure writes in the second chapter of *The Life of St Francis*, the chapter which deals with Francis' conversion:

> *One day when Francis went out to meditate in the fields, he walked beside the church of San Damiano which was threatening to collapse because of extreme age. Inspired by the Spirit, he went inside to pray. Prostrate before an image of the Crucified, he heard a voice coming from the Cross, telling him three times: 'Francis, go and repair my house which, as you see, is falling completely into ruin.'* (L 2.1)

It is equally significant that the religious journey of Francis found its completion in his experience of the stigmata on the heights of La Verna – the experience in the very depths of his being of the overwhelming love of God poured out in the crucified Christ. Francis' journey began and ended in Christ, and in order to make that journey, Francis strove more and more to imitate Christ. It was an imitation not just in externals but one which flowed from a heart filled with love for the Crucified. This was why Francis placed so much emphasis on the humanity of Jesus, without ever forgetting that the Christ who is fully human is also the God-Man. The human life which Christ lived was, for Francis, the fullest expression possible of God's love. Francis sought to imitate that life as literally as possible, in the way that the lover seeks to take on a lifestyle in conformity with the desires of the beloved. Francis' lifestyle was never an external performance. Rather, it sprang so naturally from the heart of one who was challenged by the irresistible power of God's love.

This explains, then, the centrality of Christ within Bonaventure's fundamental vision of the fulfilment of our human destiny.

The Son of God, the very small and poor and humble One, assuming our earth, and made of earth, not only came upon the surface of the earth, but indeed to the depth of its centre, that is, He has wrought salvation in the midst of the earth. (H 1.22)

It is in the way of life which is revealed in the humanity of Jesus that we are able to find directions for the completion of the journey into God. The challenge is to become Christ-like, as Francis did, to be true imitators of Christ. This is not simply a matter of imitating the actions of Christ. It is a challenge which is addressed to the heart. The challenge is to become in our whole being 'other Christs'. The moral life is not a matter of following rules and regulations but to live as Christ lived, with all the radical implications that this entails for our attitudes and duties towards God and towards our fellow human beings. Bonaventure insists that such a radical style of life is possible. Moreover, it is not only possible, but it becomes a source of true and lasting joy, it becomes the way to a happiness which fulfils every yearning of the human spirit. And this is so because it has been lived and witnessed to in the life of the poor man from Assisi.

This was shown also to blessed Francis, when on the height of the mountain, there appeared to him a six-winged Seraph fastened to a cross. There he passed over into God in ecstatic contemplation. He became an example of perfect contemplation as he had previously been of action, so that through him, more by example than by word, God might invite all who are truly spiritual to this kind of passing over. (I 7.3)

The Journey into God

In some ways we might tend to feel that while it may well be true that Francis *did* experience God, and in a very powerful way, how could it ever be possible that *we* could experience God in even remotely the same way? The world we live in is very different from the world of thirteenth-century Assisi. Moreover, Francis was an exceptional person, one of the outstanding figures of history, and his experience must have been uniquely his own. We could certainly never have the audacity to lay claim to it.

Bonaventure recognized that Francis' experience was indeed special, even unique. Yet he believed that we could all learn from Francis in order to make our own way to God. Bonaventure had applied the great power of his mind and the resources of his heart to reflection on the life of the saint, and from his meditations arose writings in which he wished to teach that not only Francis, but all who believe, are able to make the same journey to God that Francis did – even if the conditions of our individual journeys might differ. If you like, Bonaventure maps out the road and the signposts mark the various stages through which Francis himself had passed. The person who embarks on the journey with an open heart and who takes care to be attentive to the directions will reach the same journey's end as Francis did. It is part of Bonaventure's enduring genius that the path he has mapped out can also enable people of our own time to make the journey into God.

Where can this map be found and what directions does it provide? This chapter will try to find the key which will unlock the spiritual treasure of Bonaventure's path for the journey into God. It will investigate a number of his writings and in particular will examine the insights which are to be found in *Disputed Questions on the Knowledge of Christ* (in the Latin, *De Scientia Christi*).

De Scientia Christi is one of Bonaventure's more technical works. It contains seven 'disputed questions' concerning Christ's knowledge. The teaching technique of 'disputed questions' was used extensively within the medieval universities. Basically, it was a form of co-operative teaching wherein the learning process took place by means of a debate between two opposing points of view. At the conclusion of the debate, the particular question under discussion would be resolved. The title of the work indicates that in this instance, the question under discussion is that of Christ's knowledge. Bonaventure takes as his starting point the Church's belief that Christ possessed both a fully divine and a fully human nature. One of the questions that subsequently arises is this: how was Christ, in his fully human nature, able to know God who is beyond all human understanding? Bonaventure supplies an answer to this question and his answer provides exciting insights into the question of how human beings in general can come to know God. It is important to note that from the outset, *De Scientia Christi* speaks of the journey to God in terms of coming to 'know' God and that, therefore, 'knowledge' is a key concept.

Created Knowledge

The first stage of the journey is arrived at when the individual acquires what is termed 'created knowledge'. Created knowledge is the knowledge which we gain when we rationally reflect on our experience of the world around us. Bonaventure is far from sceptical about the possibility of being able to know something about the fundamental nature of our world. He accepts that human knowledge can in some way give us access to the world as it really is.

What, then, is Bonaventure's picture of 'the world as it really is'? His vision stems from his religious convictions – that all created realities originate from God and are reflections of the essential goodness of God. Consequently, if we are to understand what something *really* is, we must come to understand it in terms of where it has come from, that is, in terms of its relationship to God. The principle Bonaventure applies is a familiar one – understanding a reality in terms of its origins. When someone tells a doctor, for example, that he has a pain in his side, the doctor tries to locate its source. When the origin is found, the doctor understands the real nature of the pain and is able to treat it. Similarly with the Bonaventurean method – when the origin of created realities is found, then we can start to properly understand the realities themselves.

In order to express these religious convictions, Bonaventure employs the theological concept of exemplarism, which we encountered in the previous chapter. In this particular instance, he speaks of the 'original model' in terms of the 'eternal reason' or the 'divine ideas'.

These concepts are no doubt very foreign to the contemporary mind and it is important to unpack them. To use once more the metaphor of God as Artist, it can be said that God has prior 'ideas' of everything that appears in the created world, in the way that the artist has a prior idea of that which he or she wishes to create. When the artist reveals the idea behind the work of art, it is possible for others to come to a fuller appreciation of the work. Bonaventure argues along the same lines. If we wish to fully appreciate created realities which are God's works of art, we must seek to understand them in the light of their origin as ideas in the mind of God. It is important to remember that we are involved here with metaphorical language which cannot be applied literally to God. What Bonaventure is seeking to emphasize, however, is that in order to *know* the reality of the world around us, it is necessary to recognize that it has a transcendent, sacred dimension, since everything has come from God.

When he talks of 'divine ideas', Bonaventure does not wish to imply that all knowledge is simply planted in the human mind by God. This would do away with human responsibility and indeed would drastically restrict any concept of human freedom. Bonaventure does not look to God as the one who *determines* what we must know, imposing dictates upon us. In the Conclusion to Question IV, he speaks of God as the one who 'regulates and motivates'. As Divine Artist, God is the one who firstly regulates or brings into a certain arrangement the patterns within creation. And just as the artist desires that others should appreciate the particular nature of his or her art, reaching out and motivating them to do so, so God is the one who reaches out and motivates us to appreciate and understand the world. Bonaventure teaches that the more one grows in awareness of the presence of God, the Divine Artist, the more one will be inspired in the quest to come to a fuller understanding of the meaning and purpose both of human life and of the world around us.

The image of God *regulating* and then *motivating* is one in which God co-operates with us in our search for knowledge. In his conclusion to Question IV, Bonaventure comments: 'The principle of knowledge is to be found in the eternal reason together with the proper created reason'. Again, these appear as abstract and difficult concepts. What is Bonaventure suggesting here?

The 'eternal reason', as already noted, refers to the knowledge which God has of the whole realm of creation. As Creator, as Divine Artist, God has the deepest possible knowledge and understanding of each created entity. Human beings also have knowledge of the surrounding world. When such knowledge is gained through our experience of things, both through our senses and through our power of reflection, Bonaventure calls it 'created knowledge'. In this latter respect, Bonaventure, as a philosopher, draws upon Aristotle's teaching that human knowledge is derived from sense experience when we reason about or reflect upon that experience.

Bonaventure insists, however, that there is much more to human knowledge than what we know through the experiences gained through our senses. What we do experience through the senses is of value. But its value is not to be found when it is taken as an end in itself. Its real value lies in the fact that it becomes the means to acquiring a knowledge, a vision of the world of our experience which is so much more inspiring and uplifting than the limited vision which our senses can provide. What is experienced through the senses is to be fully appreciated, but it is not an end in itself. It is experience which is designed to lead us forward to a vision of life which is greater than we could ever have imagined.

Consider, for a moment, the appreciation of wine. The person who has never tasted wine, but who desires to gain an appreciation of wine, may begin a course in wine tasting, sampling recent vintages. The experience of wine gained in this way is real and is to be appreciated. But it is not an end in itself. This initial experience will hopefully lead the would-be connoisseur onwards to an appreciation of the great and classic vintages. It is when this latter appreciation of wine is gained that joys which were unimaginable with that first taste of wine will be experienced. So it is with Bonaventure's vision of knowledge. When we appreciate that first taste of the world around us, he claims, we do not simply have to remain content with that. It is possible to gain an ever-growing appreciation of that which we savour, a vision of life which will be the source of a joy which cannot be taken away. It is this joy which filled the heart of Francis.

Learning to Read

How, then, are we to gain such an appreciation of the world of our experiences? Bonaventure argues that 'created knowledge'– the knowledge which is gained through the experience of the world – only finds its ultimate significance when it serves the purpose of leading us closer towards God. On Bonaventure's map, all created realities are signposts which show us the way. It becomes a matter of learning to read the signs correctly.

Bonaventure frequently uses this metaphor of 'learning to read'. In other places, he speaks of the world as a 'book'. When the book is able to be read, it will lead the reader to God. Unfortunately, Bonaventure comments, there are times when human pride and selfishness bring darkness upon the earth, so that the book is unable to be read. It is only when we allow ourselves to be enlightened by God, through listening attentively and reflectively to God's revelation, that the light is provided by which, once again, the book of creation can be read.

> *When Man had fallen, this book, the world, became as dead and deleted. It was necessary that there be another book through which this one would be lighted up. Such a book is Scripture which points out the symbolism of things written down in the book of the world.* (H 13.12–13)

Creation is an important part of God's revelation. It reveals something of the mystery of God and hence is a symbol of the divine. Bonaventure points out that an attentive reading of the Scriptures will give light to our experience of the world. It will reveal that what we experience through our senses also has a transcendent dimension and can speak to us of spiritual realities. This is so even when we might least expect it. Consider one example which Bonaventure uses, the phrase in the gospels, 'be as wise as serpents' (MATTHEW 10:16). Even the often dreaded serpent is able to act as a symbol of spiritual realities. Think about the willingness of the serpent to sacrifice other parts of its body in order to keep what is essential, namely, its head. In the same way we are called to be willing to give away the non-essentials in our lives in order to preserve what is essential, which for human life is the realm of the heart, the life of love.

Bonaventure is calling us to be aware of the importance of a symbolic way of thinking in order to help us to draw closer to God.

Our world is more than just the way it appears. When we contemplate that world and reflect deeply on its symbolic significance, we shall be taught lessons of the heart and realize that life does have more than a material dimension. Bonaventure's concept of 'created knowledge' is symbolic by nature. All created things have sprung from God and confront us as enduring symbols of the presence of divine love. This was what St Francis discovered. Drawing on his inspiration, Bonaventure calls on the believer to pause and to look beneath the surface of things, to recognize the world as a reflection of God's creative goodness. The world in which we live is for Bonaventure, as for Francis, a world which, when seen in reverence with the contemplative eyes of faith, can lead us along the way towards God.

Knowing God

Created knowledge can point people in the right direction on the journey to God. The journey, however, must proceed further, and it is necessary to move deeper and deeper into the heart of the mystery. In exploring further the thought of *De Scientia Christi*, it is possible to discover additional parts of the guiding map. It is in Questions V to VII that Bonaventure more specifically addresses the question: how can human beings who are finite come to know God who is infinite?

The first point to note may appear a little technical, but it is important. In the original Latin text, when Bonaventure speaks about knowledge in Questions I to IV, he uses the Latin word *scientia*. *Scientia* refers to intellectual knowledge such as that which is gained through the study of science. In Questions V to VII, however, when he speaks of knowledge, he uses the term *sapientia*. *Sapientia* was a word which he had earlier defined as the achievement of theology, since it is a knowledge which derives from both intelligence and love. It is important to recognize that love is integral to his understanding of how we come to know God. *Scientia* is the term employed in speaking about created knowledge. When the discussion moves on to specifically discuss the nature of our knowledge of God, Bonaventure employs the term *sapientia* – which we could translate as 'wisdom'. *Sapientia*, or wisdom, is a form of knowledge which is acquired, not simply through exercising the intellect, but through the involvement of human *desire*, especially the desire of love.

In Question V, we come across another of Bonaventure's seemingly complex distinctions, that between *created* wisdom and *uncreated* wisdom. It has already been noted that the realities of the created world are able to act as symbols which can lead those who search for God closer to their final destiny. This can only come about, Bonaventure advises, when the world is encountered in a spirit of prayerful contemplation. The contemplative heart grows in the ability to recognize this symbolic nature of the world, to see beneath the surface and to appreciate, deep within, the reflections of divine love. This, for Bonaventure, is the acquisition of created wisdom.

Once this state is achieved, the human person is shaped anew, just as the lover is shaped anew in grasping the deeper significance of the gift given by the beloved. It is time now to move beyond the appreciation of the gift to appreciate the very presence of the beloved. When the human soul acquires *created* wisdom, says Bonaventure, there now exists a capacity to receive the gift of the divine presence itself – and it is the divine presence which is *uncreated* wisdom. In coming to appreciate the realities of this world as symbols of the divine love, we are motivated and directed so that it is possible to be drawn ever more deeply into the life of God. The Franciscan way to God is not to flee from the world. It is, rather, to be immersed in reverent contemplation of the world, awake with patient desire, so as to be drawn to the Source who is God.

For Bonaventure, then, coming to know God means being *drawn* to God. The one who desires God will be captivated by God, as Francis was, and in this sense *knows* God. Bonaventure emphasizes that this is the nature of our knowledge of God. Indeed, it is the only way in which the finite human person can be said to know God who is infinite.

In Question VI of *De Scientia Christi*, Bonaventure observes that it is never possible for the finite human mind to 'comprehend' God, that is to fully and completely understand God. The human mind has its limits. God is infinite, without any limits, and the finite can never fully understand the infinite. Consequently, Bonaventure comments, our knowledge of God is not to be spoken of in terms of comprehending God. We are to come to know God, not by attempting to *understand* God, but by *desiring* God. We desire that which we see as good. And since God is the highest good, God is desirable above all else. In Question VI, Bonaventure argues,

> *The soul is not satisfied with any good which it grasps and comprehends, since no such good is the highest. It is satisfied only by a good of such a sort that the soul is taken captive by its greatness and super-excellence.*

Question VII of *De Scientia Christi* provides us with a new dimension of the nature of human knowledge. It is common to identify knowledge with 'comprehension'. The type of knowledge we have of God, however, is not comprehensive knowledge, says Bonaventure. It is *ecstatic knowledge*. In using this term, he draws upon the mystical theology of Pseudo-Dionysius, but gives the concept a flavour which is derived from the experience of St Francis.

What exactly, then, is ecstatic knowledge? It is only possible to acquire ecstatic knowledge when we put aside our customary way of looking at life and have an open mind, an open heart, so that we might be able to receive a new appreciation of the significance of our circumstances. This is not a new awareness which we create ourselves. It is a new way of understanding which is given to us from beyond, it is something which happens to us. In knowledge,

which comes through ecstasy, we *know* through being drawn totally out of ourselves by the object of our desire. Our heart longs for its
beauty and we yearn to experience it in the fullest way possible.

This is the type of knowledge which Bonaventure speaks of in
relation to our knowledge of God. We prepare to receive it by firstly being willing to put aside our usual understanding of ourselves
and of the world around us. Any renewed appreciation of life is
not possible for the person who is convinced that life *is* the way
that they think it is. But when the mind and heart are not closed
but open, Bonaventure claims that it is possible to be *enlightened*.
In such a spirit of openness, which is the attitude of contemplation, the world is able to disclose itself as what it essentially is – a
radiation of the beauty of its Creator. The contemplative soul
moves beyond the discernment of God's beauty reflected in creation to grasp the very presence of the divine beauty and wisdom
itself. At that stage, the lover surrenders in ecstasy to the presence of the Beloved, 'The soul is drawn to that Wisdom in Ecstasy'
(SC 6 RESPONSE).

In the Epilogue to *De Scientia Christi*, Bonaventure describes ecstatic knowledge as 'that ultimate and most exalted form of knowledge'. It is possible to know God, not through an intellectual
process, but through the experience of God. Remaining true to
Francis, Bonaventure stresses that what is experienced is the
boundless depth of God's love. To experience this is to have certain
knowledge, more certain than any knowledge which can be
arrived at through logic. The highest form of knowledge is to be
found in the personal certainty of the love relationship. Ecstatic
knowledge finds its consummation in the experience of God. It is
this experience which Bonaventure calls 'experiential wisdom'
and it is grounded in love. What is called for here are not words
but the expectant silence of the true lover, a silence which desires
not the understanding of the idea of love, but the ecstatic granting
of divine love itself. Bonaventure concludes the Epilogue:

*This type of knowledge can be understood only with great difficulty,
and it cannot be understood at all except by one who has experienced
it. And no one will experience it except one who is 'rooted and grounded in love so as to comprehend with all the saints what is the length
and the breadth, the height and the depth ... until you are filled with
the utter fullness of God.' (EPHESIANS 3:17) And if it is to be experienced interior silence is more helpful than external speech. Therefore,
let us stop speaking, and let us pray to the Lord that we may be granted the experience of that about which we have spoken.*

In Questions V to VII of *De Scientia Christi*, Bonaventure describes
how it is possible for the human person to know God. In the first
place, our knowledge of God is not simply intellectual knowledge.
It is *sapientia*, knowledge which involves both our intelligence and
our desire to love. The first stage in coming to know God is the
acquisition of *created* wisdom. Created wisdom is gained when we
are able to approach our world in a spirit of contemplation. In
seeking the deeper meaning inherent within those realities which
confront us, we begin to discern the reflections of the Creative
Goodness. This involves movement into the second stage, when
God is firstly appreciated by the mind to be the Highest Good and
then, as the Highest Good, is desired by the heart above all else. It
is now possible to be drawn beyond ourselves through ecstatic
knowledge towards the One whom we cannot fully understand
but whom we desire from the depths of our being. In ecstatic
knowledge, the ultimate and highest form of knowledge, we gain
experiential wisdom. God gifts us with the overwhelming experience of the divine love, an experience which no words are ade-
quate to express.

Desire and love are central to Bonaventure's approach to the question of our knowledge of God. We *can* know God, claims Bonaventure. This does not entail that we can understand God – for the
finite human person, that is impossible. It is possible to know
through love, however, without having to say we fully understand.

Through love, whatever we lack is given to us; through love, an abundance of all good is given to the blessed; and through love, there is attained the supremely desirable presence of the Divine Spouse. (T 1.16)

It is, indeed, the knowledge which is the fruit of love which is the most certain of all knowledge.

The journey which Bonaventure maps out is the journey into the heart of the mystery and the attraction of divine love. It was the journey which Francis had travelled, in freedom from fear and with deep-seated joy, drawn by overwhelming desire for the beloved. It is a journey which still exerts its fascination for searching hearts within our own time. The following chapter will seek to uncover the wealth of nourishment which Bonaventure's way to God can offer to the spiritually hungry in these last years of the twentieth century.

$$\boxed{6}$$

Bonaventure:
A Spiritual Guide for Today

As we approach the third millennium, there is no sign that interest in spiritual experience has faded. Our world abounds with individuals and groups who advocate various paths for spiritual enlightenment. Sometimes, unfortunately, the avenues which people are encouraged to follow lead to false idols. We only have to witness the tragedies of Jonestown or Waco to see the disastrous consequences which emerge when the spiritual impulse is misdirected.

Bonaventure offers directions to the spiritually lost, food to the spiritually hungry. It is food which is of substance, food which will sustain and nourish those who partake of it. His spirituality is grounded in the real world. It takes proper account of our ability to reason, to imagine, to love. The journey does not leave us stranded in isolation and aridity but brings us to the springs of living water which never fail to satisfy our thirst. This living water is the boundless beauty and goodness of the God who has created us and to whom we return. Bonaventure's way to God is designed for the person who is concerned for the well-being of the world in which we live. It accepts and indeed widens the human search for knowledge. Bonaventure emphasizes the value not only of intellectual knowledge, but also of that knowledge which springs from the attitude of love. His language, the language of the literary artist as well as of the scholar, challenges our imagination, awakening in us desires for beauty and harmony, longings which find their fulfilment in God. This chapter will explore the ways in which the philosopher-theologian of medieval Paris can continue to guide the footsteps of the spiritual pilgrim of our own time.

A Spirituality of Engagement

Many of the concepts which we examined in the previous chapter suggest that in our search for God, we are not to shun our experiences of involvement with the natural world and with other people. If anything, the desire for God should bring us to value ever more deeply all that God has created and should lead not to detachment from, but to engagement with, this world of which we are a part. For Bonaventure, religion ought never to be an isolated part of life. It is not a matter of going to church to find God and then, afterwards, forgetting all that and getting on with one's real life. No, for Francis and for Bonaventure, there ought to be no separation between faith and life. The experience of God is one which has meaning within the context of all our experiences, and indeed gives deeper meaning to them.

As was noted in the previous chapter, 'created knowledge', the knowledge which we acquire when we use our ability to reason, is an essential part of Bonaventure's theory of knowledge. As an integral stage on the journey into God, created knowledge enables us to begin to know God within the context of the other experiences of our lives. In the *Itinerarium*, the knowledge which we gain through reflecting upon our experience of the world is not a hindrance to knowing God. On the contrary, when seen with the eyes of contemplative faith, it is able to lead us to the depths of the encounter with God. When the person of faith contemplates the *significance* of what he or she knows, he or she is enabled to accept the realities encountered in his or her experience as symbols of God's presence.

Bonaventure's integration of created knowledge and created wisdom demonstrate how important it is that the human individual is not thought of as an 'isolated self'. Rather, the individual is necessarily engaged with the wider world of nature and of human society. Nature is not a mundane reality to be exploited by humanity but is itself a reflection of the sacred. We are challenged to positively engage with our environment so that we, and indeed all creation, might move towards final fulfilment in God. If we seek to experience God, claims Bonaventure, our engagement with the world of nature ought to be one whereby we 'present to ourselves the whole material world as a mirror through which we may pass over to God, the supreme Craftsman' (I 1.9).

Bonaventure's understanding of the natural world and our place within it is relational and dynamic. He puts to flight any understanding of life which portrays the human person as 'the isolated individual', set in the midst of a world of passive objects, completely detached from and a stranger to the surrounding environment. Rather we are presented with a powerful, challenging vision of mutual encounter between ourselves and our world. It is a vision in which we do not simply aim to manipulate that world, but are willing to humbly acknowledge that we have much to learn from our experience of the inherent sacredness of creation.

The Moral Life

Within the Bonaventurean vision, knowledge of God has an intrinsic social dimension. It is not simply a private affair between the individual and God but necessarily entails engaging with others. Travelling along the path of the journey into God entails living a moral life, a life which will be characterized by the practice of 'virtue'. This should not be understood in terms of following abstract or impersonal obligations. Virtue, rather, is a way of life. The virtuous life is one which enables both individual and social progress along the path of the journey to God. Just as the summit of the spiritual journey is to be found in the experience of God's love, so the summit of virtue is to be found in the practice of charity.

Justice alone, Bonaventure insists, is insufficient to ensure a virtuous society. The exercise of justice will bring about a certain unity, a certain sense of order. However, if that unity and order is to last, if it is not to deteriorate into disorder and fragmentation, love is required. Each member of society ought to desire the highest well-being of the other members of society.

This ideal is no doubt difficult to achieve. Yet such a way of life is possible, Bonaventure claims, since it has been expressed in the life of St Francis. It is Francis whose experience provides a model for moral and virtuous living (H 5.5). The exhortation to live morally is a challenge to respond to the demands of divine love. It calls for a willingness to embrace, as Francis did, a way of life which will have as its foundation the values expressed in the life of Christ. Above all, the moral life is one which is caught up in the mystery of God's love for humanity, the mystery which so captivated the heart of Francis. When one's whole being is seized by infinite Love itself, one cannot but love in return.

As soon as we acquire charity, all that pertains to perfection becomes easy: acting or suffering, living or dying. We must therefore endeavour to advance in love, for perfect love leads to perfection in all else.
(T 2:11)

Our own century has witnessed many calls for justice. Sadly, it has also sometimes seen such calls degenerate into hatred, violence, mass slaughter, the imposition of totalitarian governments. Unless the struggle for justice is imbued with the fire of love, the oppressed can so easily become the oppressor and the cycle of injustice is perpetuated. Bonaventure reminds us that at the heart of morality must be found genuine love, whose source and wellspring is a love which knows no bounds – the love which flows from the goodness of God.

Bonaventure does not establish a dichotomy between our experience of God and other dimensions of human experience. His works testify to the possibility of speaking about religious experience in a meaningful manner, in terms which address the issues which arise from our necessary engagement with our natural and social world.

The Quest for Knowledge

An essential part of human endeavour is the quest for knowledge. It seems to be a part of human nature that we are continually attempting to know more – about ourselves, other people, about the world in which we live. But how we attain knowledge is also influential in determining the attitude we end up having towards that which we know. If it is thought that the objects of knowledge are just there, to be used as people wish for their own benefit, then there will be little concern for the integrity of those objects themselves. They are simply there to be exploited. To separate human knowledge from the recognition that there exists a sacred relationship between the knower and that which is known cheapens the value of human life. It was such an attitude which, in the past, allowed the flourishing of the slave trade. Individuals were treated as objects and the fundamental relational values which ought to operate in any human society were ignored. Similar attitudes prevailed in the Nazi concentration camps of the Second World War. If knowledge means investigating, from a completely detached point of view, objects 'out there', then the world which will result will be a frightening, impersonal and valueless one.

Relationship is central to Bonaventure's theory of knowledge. To truly know, he insists, is to allow the use of our intellect to be guided by the spirit of love. The challenge is to acquire knowledge in its fullest sense of *sapientia*, wisdom. To have wisdom is to be able to recognize the deepest significance of that which is before us. This requires much more than the attitude of a detached observer and investigator of facts. In order to know, Bonaventure advises, it is necessary to become engaged with that which we wish to know, and to acquire knowledge through an attitude of contemplation and reverence.

This is illustrated in his use of the term 'ecstatic knowledge'. Ecstatic knowledge is not the end product of an abstract process of investigation. It demands firstly an attitude of standing back and contemplating. Through contemplation, the knower becomes engaged with the object, is fascinated by it and desires to know it more deeply. This desire to know draws the knower into engagement with the object of knowledge and leads to an increased awareness of its significance.

Education could become so much more fruitful if the essence of ecstatic knowledge could be captured and expressed within the educational process. Too often, education can become a matter of storing up information, storing up facts – perhaps even more so in this electronic age, when so much information is available at the click of a mouse. But what is required more than information is the ability to assess the value of that information for the life of the human family. This only comes through the acquisition of wisdom. Wisdom is not acquired through speed but through depth, and it is only in contemplation that one is drawn into such depth.

Bonaventure's understanding of the essential nature of knowledge can offer inspiration to the growing number of contemporary philosophers who cry out against the negative and devastating effects of the attitude of 'disengagement' or 'detachment'. Disengagement views the human person as the investigator observing the environment from a completely detached point of view. If disengagement becomes the norm for our theories of knowledge, ultimately, it becomes destructive. If we try to develop our theories about our environment in abstraction from the people who inhabit it, we will be left with a grey and barren world, devoid of personal meaning.

There is a call to dethrone the 'disengaged Man of Reason' who is caught up in the ultimately futile belief that knowledge is only possible through objective investigation. The Man of Reason, attempting to distance the self from the object of investigation, becomes alienated from the world of *human* activity, a world which necessarily must incorporate feelings and desires. Those who protest against the Man of Reason insist that if a theory of knowledge is to be faithful, it must incorporate an attitude of contemplation. We must question what it is that we care for, what it is that we love, if we are to discover who we are, if we are to give ourselves a sense of purpose for the future.

Bonaventure would join today's protesters against the Man of Reason. The attitude of contemplation is what he called for when he spoke of 'created wisdom'. He did not reject out of hand knowledge which is gained through rational investigation – knowledge which today is commonly called 'scientific knowledge'. Indeed, he recognizes the value of scientific knowledge, labelling it created knowledge, and allocating it a specific place in the journey into God. But scientific knowledge takes its proper place when it is supplemented by accounts of other ways in which we know – knowing through contemplating, through relating, through loving.

Within the Bonaventurean perspective, to acquire 'knowledge of God' is not in the first place to know a new proposition but to experience a relationship. This is true knowledge of God, Bonaventure claims, ecstatic knowledge, and it was witnessed to in the life of Francis. What follows from this is knowledge *about* God. This is knowledge gained by reflecting upon the meaning of the experience of ecstatic knowledge and it forms the subject matter of the first six chapters of the *Itinerarium*. Such knowledge, however, steps aside in the final instance in humble acknowledgement of that highest knowledge which is found in the mystical relationship of love between the soul and God:

> In this passing over, if it is to be perfect, all intellectual activities must
> be left behind and the height of our affection must be totally trans-
> ferred and transformed into God. (I 7.4)

Bonaventure's theology offers insights for contemporary inquiry within the philosophy of religion. What type of philosophical inquiry is appropriate when approaching the question of knowing God? Perhaps the closest analogy is to be found in our understanding of how we know other people. Knowledge, however, has often been philosophically understood as that which is obtained through an attitude of critical detachment. Yet our understanding of other people naturally involves 'trust' and 'love'. If our knowledge of God is to be spoken of as in some way analogous to our knowledge of other people, then philosophers of religion are going to be forced to re-examine the philosophical understanding of knowledge and its relationship with love.

Philosophy needs to be freed from the restrictions which have been placed upon its understanding of knowledge. It needs to take into account the way people actually know. This includes, above all, that it considers the nature of the knowledge people have of each other. What then becomes clear is that there exists a reciprocal relationship between knowledge and love.

To say that we know through loving and trusting by no means entails that reason is excluded. When a person trusts someone or something, that person is said to believe in the other. Trust, however, can be misplaced. To state that I believe in some invisible person who will save my life if I step directly into the path of a speeding train can hardly be said to be a meaningful belief. It is, indeed, a dangerous belief. In order to decide whether a particular belief can be defended as meaningful for human existence, some form of rational assessment is called for. The issue of 'rationality' needs to be addressed. If a belief is assessed to be 'irrational', it could fairly be said that its value in providing meaning for human life would be discredited.

Discussion about the rationality of a belief has, however, often narrowed itself to an assessment of whether the belief accords to standards such as those formulated in the late nineteenth century by a certain W. K. Clifford: 'It is wrong, always, everywhere and for everyone to believe anything upon insufficient evidence.' According to Clifford, a proposition should be believed only when evidence can be produced which will immediately verify it.

This understanding of rational belief has been rightly questioned. Rationality pertains to *thinking persons* and Clifford's criterion is in fact quite remote from the way people actually think. Even when we are attempting to come to a conclusion on the basis of the evidence that is before us, our decision is influenced not only by the evidence but by many other prior assumptions and considerations that we bring to our assessment of the evidence.

Two historians, for example, may examine the same evidence but come to differing conclusions. We do not normally say that one of the historians is 'irrational'; on the contrary, we may hold that both positions are rational, and instead explain the varying conclusions in terms of the prior assumptions which the historians may have held and subsequently brought to their assessment of the evidence. We would only describe the conclusion as irrational if we were to make the judgement that the historians' assumptions or methods of argumentation were irrational. Such an assessment would entail a consideration of a very wide range of factors – an examination of the kind of evidence which the historian has admitted as evidence, the principles of historical interpretation followed within the tradition to which the historian belongs, and convictions about the purpose of human life which are accepted within that tradition. It will be in the light of the relationship to this wider framework that the rationality of the historian's belief that such and such was the case will be assessed.

The question of the rationality of beliefs is far wider than simply examining whether a particular proposition is justifiable according to detached and impersonal procedures of investigation. To illustrate this, the philosopher Basil Mitchell uses the example of the navigator and the lighthouse. The ship's watch believes he has sighted a lighthouse, despite the reckoning of the navigator that the ship is hundreds of miles away from land. The rationality of the watch's belief is not assessed, however, simply in isolation – his belief is wrong because the navigator's evidence contradicts it. When, a short time later, the lookout reports that he has sighted land, the watch's belief is seen to be more reasonable. We are not speaking about assessing whether an individual proposition meets the standards set by a specific investigative process – in this case, the process of navigational calculation. The rationality of a belief is to be assessed by means of an evaluation of an interacting network of factors which will defend or attack the truth of that belief.

Bonaventure's approach to the question of our knowledge of God is not structured around a process which aims to logically prove the proposition 'that God exists'. He claims, rather, that it is possible to experience God and that this experience has meaning within the context of other claims which arise from our engagement with the natural and social world. He shows that the experience of God does not cause irrational behaviour but rather has positive implications for our engagement with our environment and with our fellow human beings. Consequently his claim is acceptable in the light of other claims.

The quest for knowledge is a continuing quest. It is also one of the noblest quests undertaken by humanity. But if the quest is to be undertaken seriously, it is important to understand what we are searching for. We are not searching for mere facts – these can never satisfy the deepest longings of the human heart. We are searching for meaning, for relatedness, for that which will draw us beyond ourselves. In our search for knowledge of this kind, Bonaventure's insights can serve as a most helpful guide.

The Beauty of God

Bonaventure's writings, influenced as they are by Francis of Assisi, incorporate ways of thinking which are in keeping with the poetry and mysticism of Francis. It is not surprising, then, to find Bonaventure employing metaphorical, aesthetic language in order to capture something of the reality of the God whom Francis so powerfully experienced. The Swiss theologian von Balthasar notes the aesthetic character of Bonaventure's writings:

> *Of all the great scholastics, Bonaventure is the one who offers the widest scope to the beautiful in his theology: not merely because he speaks of it most frequently, but because he clearly thereby gives expression to his innermost experience and does this in new concepts that are his own.*

The Bonaventurean appreciation of the religious significance of aesthetic experience is illustrated in the second chapter of the *Itinerarium*. The chapter is concerned with the contemplation of God by means of what we perceive through our senses. Bonaventure speaks of 'the senses taking delight' when we experience something's 'beauty', 'sweetness' or 'wholesomeness'. This experience of delight can lead us to question what kinds of things cause us delight, and what can cause us the greatest delight. We cannot be satisfied, he claims, with finite objects as the highest cause of the sense of delight, since the experience of delight draws us beyond ourselves and our limitations. We are forever seeking deeper sources of delight. For Bonaventure, this suggests (he does not claim that it *proves*) that the ultimate source is to be found in the infinite, which is the life of God.

> *In this way that which delights as beautiful suggests that there is primordial beauty. It is obvious that in God alone there is primordial and true delight and that in all of our delights we are led to seek this delight.* (I 2.8)

Bonaventure speaks of 'the beauty of God'. It is important to note, however, that he never *identifies* our experience of God with our experience of beauty, as if religious experience can be explained simply as a variety of aesthetic experience. No – our appreciation of what is truly beautiful ought to be determined by our experience of God. Consequently, for Bonaventure, beauty can be found where many might see only its absence, for example, in Christ crucified. The crucified Christ is held up as the model of the truly beautiful because of the spiritual reality expressed there, the limitless outpouring of divine love. Beauty is not just what appears on the surface. True beauty is spiritual beauty. What makes a person beautiful is what comes from within.

> *For many are those who love beauty. But beauty is not in externals; true beauty consists in the splendour of wisdom.* (H 20.25)

When Bonaventure speaks of God as 'beautiful', he is not speaking of an abstract, conceptual beauty. God is beautiful because God is a dynamic, active God who captivates our desires, our affections, and so becomes our delight.

> *God is powerful; and if powerful, beautiful also, for wisdom is the most beautiful form: therefore God is the Wise One. 'I was enamoured of her beauty'.* (H 11.3)

Note the implications here: ultimate power is not the power of might and force but the power of attraction, the power of beauty. God does not force us into worshipping. Rather, God draws us beyond ourselves and is experienced as eminently desirable. In turn, this experience breaks in upon our normal understanding of what constitutes beauty and may radically alter this understanding. It becomes possible to discern beauty even in the darkness of the pit, even in the one who is broken and crucified.

Bonaventure's use of aesthetic language to refer to God can offer valuable insights in the quest to find meaningful ways to speak of God in today's world. Perhaps in this regard we could ponder on the distinction which Bonaventure makes in *De Scientia Christi* between *apprehension* and *comprehension*. We do not comprehend God, he says, but rather we apprehend or sense God's presence. Similarly, aesthetic experience is not a matter of comprehension but apprehension. It is impossible to analyse an experience of beauty and provide a list of logical reasons which completely explain why something is beautiful. The experience of beauty always remains more than the reasons which can be given for it. Nor does following set procedures automatically produce the experience of beauty. Rather, beauty is discovered; to use Bonaventure's terminology, it 'is sensed in some way'.

Sometimes, indeed, beauty overwhelms us, such as when we are struck by the beauty of the natural world in the overpowering majesty of a sunset, for example. In apprehending something as beautiful, we come to find it desirable. We are not involved in an intellectual exercise; it is more that we are drawn beyond ourselves and our rational concepts by that which is desirable. The language of such experience can help us to speak about God whose goodness and beauty overwhelms and captivates the one who seeks with an open and listening heart. It is language which can offer hope and meaning to those many who are growing disillusioned with the sterile world of clinical efficiency and are yearning for the eruption of the beautiful.

Bonaventure's language should not be read literally. Its aesthetic and metaphorical quality is there to lead us more deeply into the mystery of God, a God who has been experienced but who cannot be fully understood. After the stigmata, St Francis, overcome by the power of God's love, breathed this prayer to God, 'You are beautiful'. The God towards whom Bonaventure's language directs us is the God who is beautiful, the God who draws us beyond ourselves, captivates our desires and satisfies our spiritual thirst.

Authority within the Church

It is commonly held that authority is exercised within the Church because the Church is by nature hierarchical. When people think of a hierarchy within the Church, they generally tend to think of an identifiable group such as the Pope, bishops and priests who constitute *the* hierarchy. The term 'hierarchy', moreover, can often receive a bad press, since it is identified with the domination of one group over others.

This is a very static understanding of the notion of hierarchy and indeed is completely foreign to Bonaventure's use of the term. His understanding of hierarchy finds its inspiration in the writings of Pseudo-Dionysius. When Bonaventure speaks about hierarchical structures, his first concern is with the levels of spirituality *within the individual human person*. Each person is called to become 'hier-archized' in that each is challenged to grow to be 'like God' in attitudes and in actions. In the *Hexaemeron* Bonaventure comments:

> *The third part of contemplation consists in considering the hierar-chized human mind. And this is understood through the stars, or through the light of the stars, which indeed has a radiation that is constant, beautiful, and joyful. The soul, when it enjoys these three is hierarchized.* (H 20.22)

Hierarchy has its origins not in the language of power structures, but in the language of spirituality or life with God. Hierarchy is concerned with the states of being of a person in terms of relationship with God. The individual is 'hierarchized' when that person shows certain spiritual qualities and the Church is hierarchized when it enables the flourishing and expression of such qualities.

What are these qualities? To be hierarchized, according to Bonaventure's understanding, is to live the relationship with God in a way that is constant, is beautiful and is joyful. Constant, in that the spirit of prayer, of contemplation, enables one to be focused on what is truly important in life; to be attentive, to be faithful, above all to be able to love with a love that is sincere. To be beautiful, not with the beauty of the external, but with a beauty which above all grows in prayer through the acquisition of wisdom. To be joyful, in the realization that one is called by God, inspired with the power of God, a joy which expresses itself in a life of enthusiasm in service of God's kingdom.

The Church is hierarchical in nature. This does not mean that the Church has an élite who are the hierarchy. On the contrary, *all* people within the Church are called to be hierarchized. Understood in this way, the Church's hierarchical structure is not a static reality, but rather a challenge. To be a hierarchical Church should have nothing at all to do with power and domination. Any group within the Church which claims hierarchical power can only substantiate that claim if the statements issued in the name of that authority are permeated with constancy, beauty and joy, and facilitate the growth of those same attitudes within the life of the community. To speak of the Church as hierarchical is a challenge to the Church as a community to live in such a way that God's world is able to be uplifted through the witness of lives which, like the life of Francis, are constant, beautiful and joyful.

Francis, the Sultan
and Interfaith Dialogue

In this final chapter we shall be concerned with one of the pressing issues facing modern society, that of dialogue between the religions of the world. The issue of interfaith dialogue is crucial for the future of humanity. It is only when there is peace among religions that there will cease to be war among nations. And if there is to be peace among religions, religions must engage in dialogue. As was noted in chapter 1, Francis and the Sultan engaged in interfaith dialogue in the early years of the thirteenth century. There is much we can learn from the nature of that dialogue, much which can help us to develop an educational model for the continuance and enhancement of dialogue between religions in the world of our own time.

Background to the Encounter

If there are seen to be obstacles in the path of interfaith dialogue today, there were certainly no fewer obstacles in Francis' time. The meeting between Francis and the Sultan took place within the context of the Fifth Crusade. The Crusades had been triggered by the Clermont Address of Pope Urban II in 1095, which called upon Christians to defend the Christian Holy Places against the Saracens. Successive Crusades were launched throughout the twelfth century, but despite the initial success of the First Crusade, politically they proved a failure. Islam, previously divided into warring factions, grew into a powerful, united force under the challenge of

European invasion. In 1187, Saladin recaptured Jerusalem, which was for Islam, too, a holy city.

The thought of a Crusade dominated the thinking of Pope Innocent III, who became Pope in 1198. In 1212, the victory of Las Navas over the Saracens in Spain confirmed Innocent in his plan of launching a new Crusade. The following year, he announced a Council and a Crusade, and in 1215, the Council fixed the Crusade for 1217. Innocent died in 1216 and was succeeded by Honorius III who possessed similar enthusiasm for the cause of the Crusade. In 1218 the army of Crusaders landed on the coast of Egypt and laid siege to the city of Damietta. Their opponent was Sultan Melek-el-Kamil and it was with El-Kamil that Francis entered into dialogue.

The nature of the meeting between Francis and the Sultan was briefly noted in chapter 1. Jacques de Vitry, who met Francis in Damietta, speaks of Francis continuing on from Damietta, unarmed, to the camp of the Sultan. On the way, Francis was captured and taken to appear before Melek-el-Kamil. The Sultan appeared to be fascinated with Francis and listened to Francis' preaching about Christ. Finally he guaranteed a safe passage for Francis back to the Crusader camp. De Vitry records that the Sultan asked Francis to pray that he might receive from God a revelation as to which faith is most pleasing in God's sight.

The Significance of the Encounter

Whatever the historical accuracy of De Vitry's account, it is significant that an encounter between a Christian and a Muslim be described in this way at this particular time. De Vitry shared in the mentality of his time and culture, which was a Crusade mentality. He rejoiced that the 'treacherous Muslim' had been chased from Damietta in 1220. Nor would De Vitry have presented the encounter in the way that he did on account of Francis being a holy man. Perhaps the most renowned of the twelfth-century saints. Bernard of Clairvaux (1090–1153), argued that it was better to kill Muslims rather than to risk the spread of their 'wickedness'. The killing of a Muslim was not seen as a crime; on the contrary, a knight who died in battle against the Muslims could be called a martyr.

Dr Vitry's account, written before the death of Francis in 1226, in a religious and cultural environment which viewed Muslims as evil, may be held as a significant witness to the true nature of the meeting between Francis and the Sultan. We can consequently draw from this some telling points concerning interfaith dialogue.

It should be noted that when Francis came to the Muslims, he did not try to contradict the teachings of Mohammed; rather, he preached Christ. His words as recorded by De Vitry – 'I am a Christian' – drew him apart from the political conflict of his time and placed him in the world of religious dialogue. It was not only the words of Francis that created such a setting but his whole bearing. In contrast to the Crusader, Francis came to the Sultan's camp unarmed. He had left behind the world of politics and diplomacy and came openly as a person of faith.

De Vitry reports that the Sultan 'was so overwhelmed by the countenance of this man of God that he was filled with tenderness. For many days he listened most attentively while he preached to him and to his own men the faith of Christ.' The Sultan's reaction implies that Francis did not insult his religion. Certainly, there is a contrast between this setting and the account De Vitry supplies of the treatment given to followers of Francis when they departed from his model of preaching:

> As long as the Friars Minor preached the faith of Christ and the doctrine of the gospel, the Saracens willingly listened. But as soon as they openly contradicted Mohammed in their preaching, by treating him as perfidious and treacherous, the Saracens mercilessly beat them, expelled them from their city, almost massacred them.

The Sultan understood that Francis respected his religion, even if Francis told him that, from his point of view, the Christian way was more pleasing to God.

One further significant point emerges from De Vitry's narrative. Francis challenges the Sultan to go beyond the human structures and institutions which become entwined with religious belief and to seek the purity of religious faith. He challenges the Sultan to do likewise, to go beyond the Muslim political structure in order to come to terms with his own purity of faith. Although De Vitry presents the Sultan as being unable to do that, the story serves to highlight the essence of religious dialogue as being primarily concerned not with the human constructs which so often surround faith, but with the reality of what lies at the heart of religious belief.

The sources available do not allow us to gauge the extent of the impact of the meeting upon the Sultan. It is possible, however, to discern that the encounter had considerable impact upon the religious life and practice of St Francis. His writings after his visit to Egypt show that he went through an experience there which profoundly influenced his life. He is definitely struck by the religious attitudes of the Muslims, the call to prayer, the approach to a transcendent God, the deep respect for the sacred book of the Qur'ān.

The regular call to prayer proclaimed by the Muslim muezzin (crier or herald) deeply impressed Francis. In a letter to the Rulers of the People he writes:

See to it that God is held in great reverence among your subjects; every evening at a signal given by a herald or in some other way, praise and thanks should be given to the Lord God Almighty by all the people.

In an allusion to the Islamic 'salat', Francis wants the bells to be rung — the cry of the muezzin could be replaced by a bell or any other sign commonly used in the West to call people to prayer: 'At every hour and when the bells are rung, praise and honour may be offered to Almighty God by everyone all over the world'. In this way, Christians and Muslims all over the world, might be united in prayer – a powerful ecumenical sign in a society where so many were blinded by hatred for Islam.

Francis would have also observed the way Muslims prostrated themselves on the floor or with deep bows paid reverence to Allah. In a letter to the General Chapter he wrote, 'At the sound of His name, you should fall to the ground and adore Him, so that by word and deed you might convince everyone that there is no other Almighty God besides Him'. The latter expression is very similar to the Muslim 'halma': 'There is no other God but Allah'.

A deepening awareness on the part of Francis of the transcendence of God also became clear during this period. In his earlier writings, Francis had very much emphasized the humanity of Christ, as expressed in his creation of the Christmas crib at Greccio. Yet there is a clear shift towards the transcendent after his return from Damietta. In his Rule of 1221 he writes,

He alone is true God, without beginning and without end. He is unchangeable, invisible, indescribable and ineffable, incomprehensible, unfathomable, blessed and worthy of all praise.

Such language is indeed the language of transcendence. His encounter with Islam had caused Francis to ponder his understanding of his own faith the result of this was not the abandonment of his earlier faith but the emergence of a deepened sense of awareness that God was not only immanent but also transcendent.

A further illustration of the way Francis' experience of Islam affected him is found in his exhortation to show reverence towards the pages and words of the Bible. He had observed the deep respect the Muslim had for the written word of the Qur'ān, and shortly before his death in 1226 he wrote in his 'Testament': 'Whenever I find writings containing His words in an improper place, I make a point of picking them up, and I ask that they be picked up and put aside in a suitable place'. Perhaps Francis' new attitude to the world of Islam is best expressed in his Rule of 1221 when he tells his brothers who wish to go as missionaries to the Muslims that they should testify to their Christian faith not by disputation but by a simple, peaceable presence and a disposition of service.

The Encounter as a Model for Interfaith Dialogue

The faith of St Francis was deeply influenced by his experience at Damietta. A new self-understanding arose as he grew to a new awareness of his religious relationship not only with his Christian brothers and sisters but with all people. While maintaining loyalty to his own religious tradition and openly proclaiming his faith in Christ, Francis opened himself to the goodness in the Muslim tradition and faith. Thus he sought to discover a deeper, transcendent meaning in his own faith through what he had encountered in the faith of Islam. Francis came to recognize the religious meaning and truth in Islam and so commissioned his brothers to go to the Muslims not as Crusaders but as Christians, obedient and submissive to all. In his own life, Francis entered into dialogue with Islam and through reflection on his experience, he urged his example of dialogue on those who followed after him.

What principles should guide the process of dialogue? In his Rule of 1221, Francis urges that those who go to the Muslims 'avoid quarrels or disputes'. Clearly what had occurred in his meeting with the Sultan was not argument concerning human constructs or propositions. Indeed, Francis placed himself outside this perimeter and urged the Sultan to do the same. Both men became concerned with what might be called a process of 'conversion to the transcendent', to borrow a phrase from the theologian Bernard Lonergan. It implies a turning away from faith in the human constructions which often surround religious commitment to a searching for the truth which lies in the heart of ultimate reality. Such a conversion involves a letting go and a radical open-ness to the future. It means 'allowing God to be God', seeing truth not as something we already fully possess but as a reality we are yet to grasp.

What we see emerging are the conditions for proper interfaith dialogue. In the process of conversion to the transcendent, there must be a readiness to avoid domineering behaviour and to give up false ideas – as Francis did in departing from the crusading norm of his time, and as the Sultan did in granting Francis hospi-tality and a safe return. There are no conquerors or conquered, but only an attempt to come to a mutual understanding of a higher Truth. Francis became convinced that Islam, too, has its place in God's plan. Each tradition realized that the other was in touch with the divine – the Sultan asks Francis to pray for him and Fran-cis requests that Christians be united in prayer with people from all parts of the world. Dialogue has opened the way for continuing conversion to the transcendent.

The dialogue between Francis and the Sultan took place in an atmosphere of mutual respect. What may well have occurred in the first place was a respectful meeting of personalities. As individ-uals, both Francis and the Sultan were imbued with the spirit of *courtesia*, care and respect for the dignity of the other. Hence, the meeting between the two could well have been an initial meeting of spirits, a mutual respect for the identity of the other regardless of religious belief. Such respect meant that what occurred in the exchange was neither arrogant hostility nor overweening conde-scension. This basis of mutual respect allowed a wider selection of the religious world to affect one individual through the medium of another. In so doing, it allowed both to enter into the process of constructive interfaith dialogue.

What is essential in a particular religious faith can often be obscured during impasssioned theological disputes. Such con-frontations are specifically forbidden by the Qur'ān and also found no place in the life of St Francis. As we have already seen, Francis exhorted his followers to make a point of avoiding all disputation. The essential task, he insisted, is to preach faith in God Almighty (the divine attribute given special prominence in Islam) and to witness to faith by a peaceful way of living.

By stressing what is essential in the faith of Christians, Francis proclaimed the universal Fatherhood of God as the source of a spirit of universal sisterhood and brotherhood, placing himself alongside the Muslim who sees the end of humanity's search for wholeness and integration in the fundamental Reality and the fundamental Unity which is God. Dialogue between the religious faiths as to how this universal reconciliation can be achieved enables a deeper and richer understanding of what it is to be human.

Within the Christian tradition, the latter part of this century has seen considerable development in ecumenism – increased conversation, understanding and co-operation between the different Christian churches. The twenty-first century will call for an ecumenism which extends its concerns to dialogue between *all* religious groups. Dialogue occurs in an exchange of views in which we do not set out to convert the other to our own beliefs, but rather strive for a deeper understanding and knowledge of the faith which the other professes. It entails a respect for the other's beliefs and world view. Dialogue is a process which calls for more than an objective study of the external facets of a religious tradition. To understand believers from another religious community, we must attempt to look at the world, so far as possible, through their eyes. What is required, consequently, is an opening of the frontiers which divide communities in order to allow for freedom of exchange. When Francis and the Sultan opened their respective frontiers, fruitful dialogue followed.

Interfaith dialogue should result in a process of 'conscientization', whereby each faith community is awakened to a greater awareness of its own participation in the life of God who transcends all human divisions. There needs to be a mutual recognition of the 'creative need for the other', a need which is not one-sided. Just as the Christian community, for example, should strive to share the insights of Christianity, so it should seek to learn from, as Francis did, what is distinctive in other traditions. Mutual enrichment occurs when, in faithfulness to our own tradition, we are able to accept what another tradition has to teach us. Francis never disowned his Christian faith. His dialogue with the Sultan, however, enriched him and led him to invest that faith with a new and deeper meaning.

In the world of today, which sees not only divisions between nations of different religious faiths, but also friction between people of varied religious traditions who live side by side, the need for greater understanding and co-operation is great. To immerse ourselves into the environment of Damietta and to be led through the stages of this ecumenical encounter will not simply teach us about religion. It is able to create within us a greater awareness of the opportunities for dialogue within our own immediate world. The meeting between Francis and the Sultan raises such questions as the development of understanding in the light of new experience; the willingness to share life stories and to do away with preconceived and sometimes false ideas; the necessity for mutual respect in order to avoid destructive conflict; the need to identify what one essentially believes in order to truly encounter another. Refusal to enter into dialogue is a form of totalitarian self-sufficiency. Such refusal, however, since it implicitly condemns others, condemns itself. Cut off from the wellsprings of growth, there stagnation and decay can only follow. Openness to dialogue, on the other hand, proclaims confidence in the truth already experienced and a willingness to continue the journey towards the fullness of truth.

Bonaventure's theological writings may appear far removed from the setting of the religious encounter between Francis and the Sultan. It is important to keep in mind, however, that the basic structure of Bonaventure's thought has been shaped by Francis' experience of God, an experience which, in Damietta, provided the grounds for dialogue. Like Francis, Bonaventure displays a keen awareness of the presence of God in all created reality — God is not restricted to the world of the Christians. The whole world, as an outpouring of God's creative goodness, reflects the divine presence, and can lead human beings towards God. Bonaventure's theology is essentially and unchangeably Christian, but never exclusivist. Ultimately, he claims, God is beyond all concepts, all imaginings, all the words of our theological systems. Bonaventure's fundamental metaphysical principle — emanation, exemplarity, consummation — is one which can, no doubt in varying ways, be grasped by all who search for God. This is so because the principle expresses the underlying conviction that this universe, in which all have their being, is not the result of random chance but rather the outpouring of divine goodness and love. The invitation is open to all people of faith to dispense with human pride and the desire for self-sufficiency, and to pray for enlightenment. And in this spirit of contemplation it will be revealed that our world indeed radiates with glimmers of transcendence, glimmers which guide the feet of those who journey along the path towards the fulfilment of every human longing in the discovery of the source of all truth, all goodness and all beauty, which is God.

Francis, the little man of Assisi; Bonaventure, the scholar of Paris. Francis' life experience transformed the religious climate of his own time and continues to fascinate people today — people from all walks of life, people from a wide variety of religious faiths, and, indeed, people of no religious faith at all. Bonaventure breathed deeply the spirit of Francis and reflected intensely upon it. He has left us with a testimony as to the meaning of that experience for those who, like himself, are fascinated by Francis and who seek to discover the secret which will enable each of us, limited though we feel our personal spiritual resources may be, to follow the path which Francis has travelled.

Therefore, let us stop speaking, and let us pray to the Lord that we may be granted the experience of that about which we have spoken.
(SC EPILOGUE)

Notes on Sources

CHAPTER 2

The quotation from Max Scheler is from *Wesen und Formes der Sympathie,* quoted in Leonardo Boff, *Saint Francis: A Model for Human Liberation,* New York: Crossroad, 1982, 18.

Jacques De Vitry's account of the meeting between Francis and the Sultan (also cited in chapter 7) is to be found in F. De Beer, *We Saw Brother Francis,* Chicago: Franciscan Herald Press, 1983, 131–2.

Celano's *The Second Life of St Francis* (quoted on page 20) is to be found in *St Francis of Assisi, Writings and Early Biographies: English Omnibus of the Sources for the Life of St Francis,* edited by M. Habig, Second Edition, London: SPCK, 1979.

CHAPTER 4

The quotation from von Balthasar on page 35 is to be found in H.U. von Balthasar, *The Glory of the Lord: A Theological Aesthetics,* edited by J. Riches, translated by A. Louth, F. McDonagh and B. McNeil, 7 vols., San Francisco: Ignatius, 1982 91, vol. 2 (1984), 262.

CHAPTER 6

Basil Mitchell's example of the navigator and the lighthouse cited on pages 69–70 is taken from his book *The Justification of Religious Belief,* New York: Oxford University Press, 1981, 112–3. The quotation from von Balthasar on page 71 is to be found in *The Glory of the Lord,* vol. 2, 260–1.

CHAPTER 7

Lonergan's notion of 'conversion to the transcendent' (quoted on page 82) is treated in his work *Method in Theology,* New York: Herder and Herder, 1972.

Suggested Further Reading

The Writings of Francis

Francis and Clare: The Complete Works, translation and
introduction by R. Armstrong and I. Brady, The Classics of
Western Spirituality Series, New York: Paulist Press, 1982.

The Writings of Bonaventure

There are two series, each of five volumes, which provide English
translations of a large number of Bonaventure's works:

The Works of St Bonaventure, translated by Jose de Vinck,
Paterson, NJ: St Anthony Guild Press, 1960–70.
Works of Saint Bonaventure, edited by P. Boehner, M. F. Laughlin
and G. Marcil, 5 volumes, New York: The Franciscan Institute
Saint Bonaventure University, 1940–94.

The writings of Bonaventure which are relevant to this study are:

Breviloquium, translated by Jose de Vinck, *The Works of
St Bonaventure*, vol. 2 (1963).
Collations of the Six Days, The Works of St Bonaventure,
vol. 5 (1970).

De Reductione Artium Ad Theologiam, introduction and translation
by E. Healy, *Works of Saint Bonaventure*, vol. 1 (1955).

Disputed Questions on the Knowledge of Christ, introduction and
translation by Zachary Hayes, *Works of Saint Bonaventure*,
vol. 4 (1992).

Disputed Questions on the Mystery of the Trinity, introduction and
translation by Zachary Hayes, *Works of Saint Bonaventure*,
vol. 3 (1979)

The Soul's Journey Into God – The Tree of Life – The Life of St Francis,
translation and introduction by E. Cousins, The Classics of
Western Spirituality, New York: Paulist Press, 1978.

The Triple Way or Love Enkindled, The Works of St Bonaventure,
vol. 1 (1960).

Additional Reading

The widest selection of early writings on St Francis (including the
writings of Francis) is to be found in:

*St Francis of Assisi, Writings and Early Biographies: English
Omnibus of the Sources for the Life of St Francis*, edited by
M. Habig, Second Edition, London: SPCK, 1979.

The English language books that have been written on Francis
during this century are voluminous. It is unfortunate that the
same cannot be said concerning Bonaventure. It is to be hoped
that the rediscovery of Bonaventure's work within the English-
speaking world will lead to a plethora of volumes in the near
future.

A number of scholarly works are available to us, however, and
the following are recommended:

Balthasar, H. U. von, *The Glory of the Lord: A Theological Aesthetics*, edited by J. Riches, translated by A. Louth, F. McDonagh and B. NcNeil, 7 vols., San Francisco: Ignatius, 1982–91, vol. 2 (1984), 260–362.

Bougerol, J., *Introduction to the Works of Bonaventure*, Patterson, NJ: St Anthony Guild Press, 1963.

Cousins, E., *Bonaventure and the Coincidence of Opposites*, Chicago: Franciscan Herald Press, 1978.

Gilson, E., *The Philosophy of Bonaventure*, translated by I. Trethowan and F. Sheed, Paterson, NJ: St Anthony Guild Press, 1965.

Hayes, Z., *The Hidden Centre: Spirituality and Speculative Christology in St Bonaventure*, New York: The Franciscan Institute St Bonaventure University, 1992.

Index